THE PROMISED LAND

The Promised Land

*The Saga of God's Chosen People:
From Abraham to David*

Matthew E. Clancy

SERVANT BOOKS
Ann Arbor, Michigan

Published by: Servant Books
P.O. Box 8617
Ann Arbor, Michigan 48107

Available from: Servant Publications
Distribution Center
237 North Michigan
South Bend, Indiana 46601

The maps in this volume are used with permission of
C. S. Hammond & Co., New York.

Cover photo of southern Palestine taken by L. L. Orlin

ISBN 0-89283-058-1

Printed in the United States of America

To
Ted and Zula Wolfram

CONTENTS

MAP LIST

Map section follows page 206

Canaan before the Conquest
The Route of the Exodus and the Conquest of Canaan
Canaan as Divided among the Twelve Tribes
The Empire of David and Solomon

Introduction

Today, as in the past, there are many whose search for God leads them to the Bible. It is often difficult, however, to recognize the good news that the pages of scripture contain, for the Bible is not a simple narrative of events. On the contrary, the historical events recorded there lie separated from one another in the various books. Hence the continuity of the story is interrupted and the significance of this or that important happening may elude the inquirer, causing him to lose track of the trend of God's work among men. This is all the more likely to take place because the recital of that story is often overlaid with a mass of complex, additional information that hinders the narrative flow.

The object of *The Promised Land* is to throw into high relief the majestic story of God's revelation of himself to mankind, and his action in forming and raising up a people during the first thousand years of established biblical history. It does this by unraveling the knot of recorded facts that make up the background of the scriptural narrative, imparting to them unity and clarity. The momentous events that compose this narrative are arranged in sequence, that is, in their actual chronological progression.

Supplemental detail is passed over, and there is a shying away from whatever interferes with or delays the telling of the sacred history itself. This includes explanatory and parenthetical observations, repetitions of statement and duplications of passages, and other distractions from the narrative as such. Digressions that anticipate future happenings and continuities that were postponed but are resumed or recapitulated at a later date are gathered together and placed in their proper historical setting. Set forth thus starkly, the message of salvation contained here can hardly be mistaken by any earnest searcher.

In these thousand years we see unfold before us a vision of God's dealings with the world in the late Bronze and the early Iron Ages. It should be kept in mind that man was then still young in terms of what is commonly called "civilization." Yet God chose this time to intervene in human history, and he chose the Hebrews —a people even less accomplished in certain respects than their neighbors—to be a nation specially consecrated to himself. He dealt with them just as they were at the time—a rude but developing people, whose particular destiny was to cling to a revealed monotheism and gradually grow in comprehension of the divine attributes. They slowly came to understand that the wrathful, awesome God whom they had learned to fear was also loving, compassionate, and merciful. They needed time in order to fully grasp a truth so tremendous.

In this era the Bible recounts the great events of the Patriarchal, Mosaic, and Davidic periods. It traces the history of God's Chosen People, the Hebrews, from the days of the Patriarchs through the Egyptian captivity and the exodus. It then follows that nation through the conquest of the Promised Land and the disorganization that ensued there. In time we encounter David and witness the formation of his kingdom. Finally, we arrive at the beginning of the reign of Solomon.

The pervading theme of these centuries is that of persevering faith, faith in the ever-present patronage of God and in his promises.

The Patriarchs believed in a divinely-revealed though distant future, while confident that God was continually in touch with their own lives. We perceive Abraham's faith, both when he was called to believe God's promise of an heir and when he was called upon to sacrifice that heir. We hear of "God's kinsman," Isaac, who trusted in the efficacy of the Patriarchal blessing to endow and bless generations to come. We witness Jacob-Israel's faith in God's custodial protection of himself, his twelve sons, and their destiny. Joseph's faith that God had used him as an instrument to preserve the progeny of Israel shines forth as well. The nation founded by Moses believed that God was dealing directly with them as his Chosen People. We observe the faith of the emancipator Moses and the Israelite tribes joined with him in ratifying a solemn, mutual covenant with the Lord their God. The period ends with David, who believed that God had anointed him as king in order to prepare the building of a Temple dedicated to the Lord. David himself was devoted to the Lord in a faith that was humanly imperfect, yet lived in prayer and ritual worship.

No liberties are taken with the Word of God in *The Promised Land*. But the findings of the sciences—the discoveries of archaeologists, the conclusions of historians, and the light shed by linguistics—are utilized to render the synthesis of the story orderly and complete. Maps are inserted to help fix the locations of major happenings. Documentation and bibliography of the volume's contents are found in the pertinent books of the Bible: the Pentateuch, Ruth, 1 and 2 Samuel, 1 Kings, 1 and 2 Chronicles, the Psalms, Ecclesiastes, and Ecclesiasticus. The Hebrew, Septuagint, and Vulgate texts of these books have been diligently consulted.

The earliest chapters of biblical history as reproduced in *The Promised Land* make a fascinating story, far superior to a literary thriller in nature and a rival of it in suspense. Recounted in unity and with clarity, this age-long quest for salvation is a thing of vivid, shining glory, truly monumental in its impact.

Matthew E. Clancy, S.T.D., Ph.D.
Swanton, Ohio

CHAPTER ONE

ABRAHAM

Genesis 1—25; 1 Chronicles 1:1–33

The Pre-Biblical Ages

The human race has no memory of its birth and infancy. But anthropology has been able to shed some light on those unremembered times when mankind lived as a nursling for an interminable age. Archaeologists, sifting through the debris deposited during this vanished era, have unearthed rude artifacts, presumed to be the earliest made by man. These were discovered in certain low-lying strata that were deposited during what anthropologists term the Neolithic Age, 5,000 years before Christ.

By 5000 B.C. man was leading a sedentary style of life, dwelling in hut villages. A scattered few of these centers of human habitation have been discovered in such far distant loci as Antioch in Syria, Jericho in Palestine, and Deir Tasa in Egypt, but most of them were found clustered in Mesopotamia. There in the land between the rivers, on the rich loam of great bottomlands in the alluvial plains of the valleys of the Euphrates and the Tigris, *homo sapiens* crawled from his cradle, to straggle through adolescence and reach maturity as civilized man. The first traces of culture have been uncovered in excavations made along the lower Euphrates at Shuruppak, Urak, Kish, Nippur, Ur, and Susa, together with some others made along the upper Tigris at Nuzu, Kirkut, and Nineveh.

Ethnically, the people of the Mesopotamian region were non-Semitic. They named their land Sumer and called themselves the Black Heads. The men, typically, were wavy-haired and full-bearded; they dressed in sheepskin kilts and left their torsos bare.

In their settlements have been found certain small stone cylinder seals which were used to roll out impressions in relief onto the surface of moist clay that was then baked. Genuine writing—a slightly later historical development—has been found there in the form of rude pictographic script, as well as in the form of more advanced, refined cuneiform alphabetic characters. These primitive records present a readily intelligible account of the culture of that age.

In the closing years of the fourth millenium B.C. these literate peoples drew together in powerful aggregations under the rule of dynastic kings. They built vast networks of canals to irrigate their countrysides. Their domesticated animals, herds of cattle, and flocks of sheep were able to graze there and grow fat. In their city-states, they built great tower temples—ziggurats—which were meant to serve as pinnacles for their gods. Rising up from the Sumerian flatlands, the tall ziggurats dominated the cities. Not a few of the towns possessed libraries of thin, flat, burnt clay tablets, all cuneiform-inscribed. Each library contained in tablet form a store of literary collections telling of the land's history and traditions. Scribes used a three-sided prism pressed into the surface of soft clay to do this writing. The written tablets had three vertical columns on both sides which were read from left to right.

By 2500 B.C. the Sumerians had been superseded, however, by the waves of Semitic invaders who washed into Mesopotamia from Arabia—the Amorites, or "Westerners." United under a king named Sargon, these newcomers assimilated the extant ancient culture, but introduced their own language to communicate it. Although they renamed the country Akkad, they preserved three of the primeval traditions: a disorderly creation story; tradition of ten fabled antediluvian kings, paralleling the Bible's list of ten Patriarchs from Adam to Noah; and the story of a universal deluge, reworked by innovative Akkadian genius. The last of these they furbished with great skill, turning it into man's first literary masterwork, the famous Epic of Gilgamesh.

In the Epic of Gilgamesh the Akkadian Utnapishtim replaced the Sumerian Kiusudra, both names meaning "day of life prolonged." Utnapishtim was a legendary priest-king of Uruk, central city-state of the lower Euphrates, who was celebrated as the "Immortal Man." He had built an ark which was 120 cubits square and seven decks high, each deck having nine rooms; and by means of this ark he had saved the human race from drowning in a sea of waters blanketing the earth. His ark survived six days and nights of unrelenting, tempestuous rain and finally grounded itself on Mount Nizir. Utnapishtim then sent out in succession a dove, a swallow, and a raven. For this exploit Utnapishtim was hailed as "the savior of all living things and of the seed of humanity." He was given the reward of a life like that of the gods, his soul being made immortal; and he was renowned thenceforth as the priest-king savior. He dwelt far away on Mount Dilmun.

There is some likeness between Utnapishtim and the Bible's Noah. Noah's ark was 300 cubits long, thirty cubits wide, and three decks high. It saved all the living animal species from extinction by safeguarding two (one male, one female) of each kind, and it drifted under torrential rains for forty days and forty nights on flood waters covering the earth. The ark grounded on Mount Ararat, and Noah sent out a raven once, and a dove three times. Though not made immortal, Noah was granted an enormously long life of 950 years.

Gilgamesh had descended from the same legendary line of kings as Utnapishtim. Longing to be made immortal like his ancestor, he shrank from the thought of oblivion. Gilgamesh was inconsolable when Enkidu, once a rival but later an intimate friend and companion, turned to clay (Akkadian euphemism for died). "My friend has become clay. Am I to sleep like that? Am I never to rise up through all eternity?" He yearned to converse with Enkidu and thought to embark on a quest of the heavenly heights. Shamash, the sun-god, warned him, "the life you seek you shall not find"; and Ishtar, goddess of love and fruitfulness, urged him to resign himself to a mortal's life on earth, and gave him counsel equivalent to "Eat, drink, and be merry, for tomorrow you will die."

Where are you bound, O Gilgamesh?
The life you seek you shall not find.
   When the gods created man,
   It was death they reserved for him,
While they retained life within their own hands.
So, fill your belly, Gilgamesh.
   Be merry day and night.
   Live joyfully every day,
Dance and make music all the time;
Launder your garments, shampoo your hair,
   Bathe yourself all over;
   Cherish the child in your lap
And, rejoicing, take your wife to your bosom.
For the life you seek you shall not find.
   That is man's destiny,
   Which can nevermore be changed.

These excerpts are quoted in *Light from the Ancient Past* (p. 28),
by Jack Finegan. They come from an old Babylonian version
of the Epic.

Many long years later, the sardonic ring of these passages was
still resounding, with the author of the Book of Ecclesiastes ex-
claiming:

Go, eat your bread all joyfully,
And drink your wine with a merry heart:
Now is when God favors your works.
Be dressed in white all of the time,
And spare not scented oil on your head.
Yes, pass your life with the wife you love
Through all the fleeting days of your life.
For that is the lot assigned to you
For your toil and labor here under the sun.
Whatever you hoped to turn your hand to,
Do it now while power is yet left to you.
Neither work, nor reason, nor knowledge, nor wisdom—
None of those things at all will there be
In the nether world to which you are going. (Eccl 9:7–10)

Saddened, and still hungering for everlasting life, Gilgamesh determined that he would make a pilgrimage to the far and almost inaccessible shrine of the immortal Utnapishtim. It meant a seemingly endless and agonizing journey, full of hazards, and involved the crossing of a wilderness of streams and mountains. Crazed with grief and dreading the specter of death, Gilgamesh persevered and overcame all obstacles, finally arriving at the shrine known as the isle of the blessed. There the Immortal One welcomed him. In order to explain why he had received the gods' gift of an eternal soul, Utnapishtim recounted at length the story of the deluge. His immortality, he said, was a personal prerogative which Gilgamesh could not hope to share. As Utnapishtim did not wish to deprive Gilgamesh of all hope, however, he sent him to get a cutting from the root of the thorny, rose-colored plant of life. After he had obtained it, Gilgamesh departed, only to have the sweetly fragrant root stolen and eaten by a serpent. In one version, the Epic concludes with the scene of Gilgamesh, still bitterly haunted by the fear of death, speaking with the ghost of Enkidu through an opening to the nether world. Gilgamesh prayerfully beseeches one of the gods for permission to speak with his dead friend:

O Utu, I would speak with you,
I beg you please give heed to my word.
   In my city when a man dies,
   Hearts are heavy and dejected
At his passing. I have climbed the dike
And seen corpses floating on the river.
   Am I to be served like that?
   A man's tallness is never up
To reaching the skies, nor his amplitude
Ever so great as to cover the earth.
   Since no brick has yet been stamped
   With the mark of my fated end,
Only let me course the length of this land,
And I will everywhere blazon your name.

His prayer was heard, and the desolate ghost of Enkidu appeared. But he said to Gilgamesh, "Do not touch me; friendship cannot last forever." Enkidu found no enjoyment in the afterlife and would have preferred to remain on earth.

The Settlements at Ur and Haran

The ruins of Ur have now been buried for 4,000 years, and are covered to a depth of eight feet by alluvial clay. Archaeologists who have dug down and exposed its remains describe the town as it existed around the year 2000 B.C. A walled city thirty-five miles downriver from Uruk, it occupied an island formed by the Euphrates to the east and a grand canal to the west, where it sat on a brickwork platform designed to keep it raised above flood stage. It had a quarter of a million inhabitants, who worked and lived in flat-topped, two-storied brick buildings lining a maze of lanes for streets. From the grand canal ran scores of smaller canals that branched out across the plain, sluicing the life-giving water through the countryside and irrigating its fertile soil. As far as the eye could see, there would have been vegetable gardens, fig and pomegranate groves, the green fields of farms, and hamlets fringed with date palms.

For several centuries preceding this date, as has been said, the Semitic Amorites had been sweeping out of the Arabian Desert into Mesopotamia in whirlwind gusts of conquest, and had then settled down to ingest and absorb, but also to reinvigorate the effete Akkadian civilization. As they assimilated this treasure trove of cultural refinement, the moon god still reigned atop the ziggurats of the city-states, and polytheism and polygamy prevailed as a normal part of life. It is at this place and time that the Bible narrative begins to be substantiated history. It is likely that the biblical figure Terah (Gn 11:27–32) with his sons and their wives had been residing at Ur for some time before the founding of the third dynasty of Ur. This would be the middle of the Bronze Age, somewhere close to 2000 B.C. Terah is proudly recorded as a direct descendant of Shem, son of Noah. Terah's household comprised his three sons, Abram, Haran, and Nahor; and Haran's son, Lot; and Haran's two daughters, Milcah and Iscah. Abram had married Sarai, his half sister (Terah's daughter by another marriage). Nahor had married his niece Milcah. No children or concubines are mentioned, but it is said that Haran, Lot's father, died at Ur.

The sacking of Ur is thought to have taken place at about 1960 B.C. This was the event which led to the establishment of the third dynasty, with Ur-nammu proclaiming himself "King of Sumer and Akkad." Perhaps, though there is no concrete evidence in confirmation, the threat of such a happening or the alarm at its taking place led Terah and his household to emigrate to Haran. Depending on the presumed date of the fall of Ur and his later, stated age at the time of God's call, Abram would then have been about fifty years old. He was childless, Sarai being barren. In following the caravan route for 600 miles to the northwest through the upper Euphrates valley, they would have had to pass through the kingdom of Mari and into the province of Paddan-Aram in order to settle at Haran on the bank of the Balikh tributary of the Euphrates.

Haran was situated at the apex of what historians and scripture scholars aptly call the "Fertile Crescent"—that belt of verdant land which extends from the delta of the Euphrates to the delta of the Nile, and which conjoined the oldest civilized centers in the Middle East. North of the barren sands of the vast Arabian Desert, the Fertile Crescent arches in the shape of a quarter moon, forming a huge tract of inhabitable and arable land. This area was a throbbing artery of traffic between the nations, the scene of mercantile exchange and wars of conquest. For centuries, caravans shuffled back and forth there over crisscrossing routes that linked settlement to settlement, while rival armies engaged each other in power plays. The eastern sector of the Fertile Crescent comprised the whole Mesopotamian valley of the Euphrates; its western took in the Mediterranean coastal lands of Syria, Lebanon, Palestine, and the lower Nile valley. It was this western sector that would be the stage for the Bible's cast of historical personages. The peoples of the Crescent were Semitic races but for a few exceptions (such as the Hittites of Asia Minor and the Medes beyond the Tigris). Terah and his offspring were probably *Habiru,* that is, Hebrew Aramaeans, and spoke Aramaic.

Since they lived in the midst of a brisk commerce passing through Haran (a name which means "caravan"), it could be that Abram and Lot served either as leaders of caravan trains or were associated with a local caravansary. They were, at any rate, under the influence of that settlement's trekking bands of traders with their retainers and bondsmen, their filing herds of donkeys, oxen, and camels, and their milling flocks of sheep and goats. Although Terah's household probably did not reside in the town proper, they would have done business with the caravans in the open country. In that case, their headquarters might well have been on the town's outskirts and subject to the influence of the pagan milieu. As Joshua was to remind the Israelites more than six centuries later, "In ancient days your ancestors lived beyond the river, such as Terah father of Abraham and Nahor. And they served other gods" (Jos 24:2).

It was here at Haran, in a land of many gods, that the Lord God now spoke to Abram. In all recorded human history this was the first instance of the divine voice being heard by man:

Go forth from the land of your kinsfolk,
And from your father's house;
Venture forth to the land I will show you,
Where you will be made a great nation,
And you will be filled with my blessings.
I will make your name be great,
And your very person be hallowed.
Them that bless you I bless,
And I will curse those who curse you.
All nations on earth will know
That blessing is found in you. (Gn 12:1–3)

Tradition among the Hebrews was superlatively clear and astoundingly tenacious. One thousand years later the words God spoke to Abraham were set down in Gn 12:1–3 by the "Yahwistic" compilers and "Elohistic" editors in the time of David.

That the year 1935 B.C. is the approximate date of the divine summons to Abram seems to be verified by collating numerous passages in Genesis with Ex 12:40. The Bible, in Genesis (12:4;

21:5; 25:26; 47:9), sets down with careful precision time observations that total 215 years as the time spent by the Patriarchs in Canaan, that is, the time stretching from Abraham's arrival there to Jacob's entry into Egypt.

To definitely establish, as far as possible, the start of the Patriarchal period in Canaan, the archaeologist Jack Finegan in *Light from the Ancient Past* offers a plausible resolution of the much-disputed question of the length of the stay of the Israelites in Egypt.

As to the length of time the children of Israel (Jacob) were in the land of Egypt there are two traditions. The first represents this period as covering 430 years, or in round numbers 400 years. The precise figure of 430 years is given in the Hebrew text of Exodus 12:40f. (P), "Now the time that the children of Israel dwelt in Egypt was four hundred and thirty years" . . . The second tradition as to the length of time the Israelites were in Egypt appears in the Septuagint version of Exodus 12:40 which reads, "Now the time that the children of Israel dwelt in Egypt *and in the land of Canaan* was four hundred and thirty years." Since, as we have seen, the patriarchs were in Canaan for 215 years, this would allow the Israelites only 215 years in Egypt. . . . In this case, the Hebrew text of Exodus 12:40 seems more reliable than the reading in the Septuagint. The fortieth verse states that the Israelites were in Egypt 430 years. The forty-first verse continues, "And it came to pass *at the end of four hundred and thirty years, even the selfsame day it came to pass,* that all the hosts of Jehovah went out from the land of Egypt." In this context, verse 41 is a very impressive affirmation. After 430 long years of life and bondage in Egypt the Israelites finally found deliverance. When verse 40 is rendered according to the Septuagint, however, the point of verse 41 is largely lost. . . . Of the two traditions which represent the Egyptian sojourn as enduring for either 430 or 215 years the former is the more strongly supported. If we accept this view and take the figures as they stand, the patriarchs were 215 years in Canaan and the Israelites were 430 years in Egypt. Abraham entered Canaan, then, 645 years before the Exodus. . . . Taking the more probable date of 1290 B.C. for the Exodus and adding the figure of 645 years which was just arrived at as the better supported tradition for the period from the Exodus back to Abraham, we arrive at the date of 1935 B.C. for Abraham's entry into Canaan. (pp. 58–60, italics mine)

Since Abram was seventy-five at the time of his call, it would seem to follow that he was born at Ur in 2010 B.C. or thereabouts. With implicit trust in God's words, he did go forth, and thus became the man of faith that he was ever afterward renowned to be. The "great nation" that God was to make of him would be called the "Israelites," the descendants of Abraham's grandson Jacob-Israel.

Abram's Passage through Canaan to Egypt and His Return

The Promised Land is about the size of modern Belgium or the state of Maryland. Approximately 150 miles long, it is as narrow as eighteen miles at its northern extremity but considerably wider, as much as seventy miles, in the south. From the plains of the Mediterranean seacoast the land of Canaan rises up onto the foot-hills, valleys, and eminences of a low mountain range that consti-tutes a central highland. The greatest elevation is 3,000 feet near Hebron. To the east, that highland overlooks the deepest gash in the earth's continental surfaces—the Great Rift. This chasm starts in the foothills of Mount Hermon, plunges down the Jordan river valley into the Dead Sea, then continues through the Arabah into the Gulf of Aqaba. The rift's deepest point is the bed of the Dead Sea, where it drops to the colossal depth of approximately 1,500 feet below sea level. The Dead Sea has no outlet and is charged with salt and bituminous particles. Its northern end, opposite 3,000-foot Mount Hebron, is about 200 feet deep. The southern end is shallow, becoming a swamp which was once the site of Sodom and Gomorrah.

Apart from its highland-lowland contrast, the country of Ca-naan presents other marked diversity: low rocky mountains, syca-more-forested valleys, grassy and rolling hills, plains of lush green or blooming growth, stretches of stagnant swamps, and arid wastelands (the biblical wildernesses).

At the time of Abram's entry into Canaan, the country belonged to the native peoples, but was also a quasi-protectorate of the Egyptian empire's twelfth dynasty. The land was sparsely populated outside of the coastal towns; there were only a few scattered settlements at stations on the caravan routes that traversed the highlands. Roving bands of Hittites from the north had infiltrated the highlands, however, and questing Amorites from the south had infiltrated the lowlands.

On his way toward the Promised Land, Abram and his household probably chose the caravan route that slanted southwest to Damascus. After fording the Euphrates, with snow-capped Mount Hermon (8,000 ft.) on their right, Abram and his companions would have taken the ancient road later named the "king's highway." They soon left this road, probably turning right in the valley of the Jabbok. Once they had crossed the Jordan and climbed westward into the highland of Palestine, they made camp on the valley floor at Shechem, with Mount Gerizim (2,849 ft.) on their left and Mount Ebal (3,077 ft.) on their right. At this almost prehistoric caravan station, God appeared to Abram and said that he would give the land to Abram and his descendants. The travelers continued southward through the mountains for about twenty miles and pitched camp between Ai and Bethel. There Abram built an altar and called upon God. By stages they then traveled across the highlands and down into the southern hills and valleys of the Negeb (a word meaning "south country"), where under normal conditions they would have encountered wells and oases. At this time, however, the region was dried up and famine prevailed. Abram and Lot, with their household and property, were therefore driven to go beyond the Promised Land.

Heading west across the 200 mile stretch of the Shur wilderness, they sought to find refuge in the lush grazing lands of the Nile valley. The Egyptian border was protected by the stout fortifications of the "Princes' Wall." Permission from the Pharaoh and, no doubt, the payment of an entry fee would have been required there for passage on to Memphis and such Egyptian wonders as the Pharaoh's palace, the pyramids, and—of vital interest to

them—the land's verdant pastures. How long the Patriarch stayed
in Egypt we are not told. Clearly, his intention was to wait for
conditions to improve in Canaan. At this time Egypt was in its
middle kingdom; the reigning Pharaoh was perhaps Amenemhet
I, of the twelfth dynasty.

Praise of Sarai's striking beauty came to the Pharaoh's ears. Out
of fear that his life would be jeopardized if he became known as
Sarai's husband, Abram introduced her to the Pharaoh simply as
his sister and not also as his wife. She was indeed his half sister,
since both were children of Terah by different mothers. As he later
explained to Abimelech, kinglet of Gerar, "She's the daughter of
my father by a mother different from mine" (Gn 20:12). Since
Sarai was ten years younger than Abram, the story was convincing
enough; the Pharaoh thought her unmarried and took her into his
palace. He then showered upon the Patriarch gifts of flocks, oxen,
donkeys, camels, and both male and female slaves. But God suddenly afflicted the Pharaoh and his whole household with a dreadful plague. Upon discovering that his troubles came of having
taken Abram's wife, the Pharaoh restored Sarai to her husband
and withdrew his favor from them. The Hebrew squatters were
driven out and escorted back to the frontier forts of his realm.

Abram and Lot Go Apart

Abram indeed had prospered. He was immensely more wealthy
now than when he had entered Egypt: Besides silver and gold, he
had slaves and valuable livestock. He led his people and his animals back across the steppes of the Shur to the region of the
Negeb, returning thence by stages to Bethel. There where he
had built an altar between Bethel and Ai, Abram called again
upon God.

By now the great quantity of tents, herds, and flocks had begun
to pose a problem. The combined herds of Abram and Lot were
making an intolerable demand upon the grazing fields, and the
herdsmen of the two camps had fallen to quarreling with one
another. If they were to live in peace, the Patriarch decided that
the two companies would have to separate.

Generously, Abram allowed Lot to choose the lands where he desired to settle, and promised that he himself would take the opposite direction. About them stretched the highlands, while to the east lay the lush Jordan plain. Lot chose the watered lowland. He parted company with Abram and pitched his tents near Sodom in what is now part of the southern end of the Dead Sea. The territory selected by Lot included Gomorrah as well as Sodom. The inhabitants of both these cities were addicted to depraved and unnatural practices.

After the two camps had separated, God spoke to Abram for the second time.

Look about you! Look north, south, east, and west.
   To you and to your descendants
I intend to give this land for ever;
   And I will see that your offspring
Are as countless as are specks of dust on the ground,
   Exceeding man's power to number.
Go, traverse the length and breadth of this land,
   Since I mean to give it to you. (Gn 13:14–17)

Abram moved on and sojourned in the valley of the Amorite Mamre. Mamre and his two brothers, Eschol and Aner, became adherents of the Patriarch. The Valley of Mamre, where a celebrated oak tree suggests that the place might once have been the site of a sanctuary, was a valley that lay about two miles north of Hebron along the east side of the road to Jebus (later Jerusalem). Abram's encampment stood at dead center in the highlands that hang above the deepest part of the Jordan valley.

During Abram's stay the region below suddenly became the scene of an incursion. The invaders, attempting to put down a revolt of Sodom and Gomorrah, seized and sacked those cities, carrying off Lot, his people, and his belongings in the process. A survivor brought news of the disaster to Abram and his Amorite allies at Mamre. Upon hearing what had happened to his nephew, Abram mustered his forces: 318 men-at-arms among his bondsmen, vassals, and confederates. They hastened off in pursuit, going up northward on the other side of the Jordan along the king's

highway. Somewhere near Laish (the Dan of later times), Abram
fell upon the rear of the retreating raiders, harried them to a point
north of Damascus, and obtained a complete victory. As Abram
was passing through the Valley of Shaveh on his way home,
bringing with him Lot and all his kinsman's household, he was
met by some of the chieftains of the Jordan plain. The king of
Sodom offered to pay tribute, but Abram declined any remunera-
tion other than for the expense of his men-at-arms. This was the
occasion, however, for the meeting of Abram and the Amorite
ruler of Salem (or Jebus) named Melchizedek. Since he was a priest
of God Most High, Melchizedek made a communion offering of
bread and wine, and blessed Abram with these words:

> Blessed be you, Abram, by God Most HIgh,
>> The creator of heaven and earth!
>> And blessed be God Most High,
> Who has handed your enemies over to you! (Gn 14:19–20)

God Makes a Covenant with Abraham

While at Mamre, Abram had a vision in which he and God
spoke with one another.

> Be fearless, Abram, for I wilı protect you.
> And yours is to be a surpassing reward.
>> "Lord, grant me a request: I have no descendant;
>> You have never given me a child.
>> Eliezer, my steward, will be my heir."
> Your heir shall be of your own flesh and blood.
> Look up at the sky and count the stars;
> Just so shall your descendants be.
> I am the Lord God, who brought you out
> Of Chaldean Ur, that I might transfer
> This land to you and your possession.
>> "How will I know that I will possess it?"
> Go bring me a three-year old heifer, and then
> A three-year old she-goat, a three-year old ram,
> A turtledove, and a pigeon that is young. (Gn 15:1–9)

Abram had shown himself to be a man of faith ever since God spoke to him at Haran. He believed in God's promises, and this faith rendered him upright in God's sight. The Lord was now about to make a covenant with him.

When Abram had brought the animals he cut them in two (except for the fowl) and arranged the halves in two lines, each half opposite its counterpart, and drove away the birds of prey which tried to alight on them. The ritual of covenant-making required the pledging parties to pass between the slain animals as a sign of formal recognition that violation of the covenant would be punishable by death. As twilight fell, Abram was seized with a sense of horror and gloom, and passed into a stupor. God spoke to him again:

Be aware your descendants will certainly be exiles
In a land not their own, where they will be enslaved,
Suffering oppression for four hundred years.
But I will pass judgment on the enslaving nation,
And they will escape with many possessions.
Yourself you shall go to your fathers in peace,
And you will be buried at a ripe old age.
Those others shall return here in the fourth generation,
Though Amorite wickedness will not yet have ended. (Gn 15:13–16)

When the sun set, a smoking brazier and a firebrand appeared and passed between the halves of the carcasses. God then made a covenant with the Patriarch.

To your descendants I give this land,
From the Wadi Egypt to the great Euphrates,
With its Kenites, Kenizzites, Kadmonites, Hittites,
Perizzites, Rephaim, Amorites, Canaanites,
Its Girgashites, and its Jebusites. (Gn 15:18b–21)

Though the Covenant was now in effect, Sarai remained barren. As she had been unfruitful in Canaan for ten years, Sarai decided to present Hagar, her Egyptian slave-girl to Abram as a concubine.

In line with the Mesopotamian custom, a child conceived by Hagar could be claimed by Sarai as her own.

When the concubine had become pregnant, however, she began to put on insufferable airs. Sarai complained to Abram and was given leave by him to do as she wished to Hagar, whereupon she proceeded to make life so miserable for the slave-girl that she ran away. When Hagar had gotten as far southward as Lahai Roi on the road to the Shur wilderness, an angel appeared to her, bidding her to return to Sarai and name her son Ishmael. Ishmael, the angel said, would be a wild-ass of a man, but his descendants (the Bedouin tribes of the Arabian Desert) would become numerous past counting. Since Abram was eighty-six years old at that time, Ishmael's birth was probably about 1924 B.C.

Thirteen years later God appeared again and spoke to Abram. In token of the Patriarch's now-closer relationship with him because of the Covenant, God disclosed a proper name by which he could be addressed. The name revealed then was "El Shaddai," which actually means "Mountain God," but which has usually been interpreted and translated as "Almighty God." At this time the Lord also changed the names of Abram and Sarai to Abraham and Sarah.

I, El Shaddai, am God Almighty.
Walk before me without offense.
There is a Covenant between us two.
Now, then, I have covenanted that you
Will become the father of many nations.
Henceforth let Abram not be your name;
Let it now be pronounced as Abraham,
Since you will be father of a host of nations.
I will render you exceedingly fertile:
Peoples and kings shall stem from you.
This Covenant drawn between me and you
And all your descendants after you
Must be everlastingly maintained.
I am to be your and your offspring's God,
And you are to be given this land where you stray,
The land of Canaan in its whole extent,

As your and their possession for ever.
Accepting the fact that I am your God,
You shall maintain my Covenant,
As after you will all your descendants.
Your males, one and all, are to be circumcised,
The flesh of the foreskin excised in token
Of this Covenant existing between you and me.
All your eight-day old boys must be circumcised,
Every male child of each generation—
Those born in the household, as well as those bought
Or acquired from aliens, hence not of your blood.
My Covenant is thus marked for good on the body.
Any male whose foreskin is not so excised
Is cut off from his people, the Covenant broken.
As for Sarai your wife, she shall now be called Sarah.
I will bless her and give you a son by her.
I will bless him in turn, so that thus from him
Nations will descend and kings will be born. (Gn 17:1–16)

"El Shaddai" was the name by which the Patriarchs were to call
upon God until he revealed another name, "Yahweh," to Moses
at the beginning of the exodus.

Abraham's Promise of a Son by Sarah

Abraham had been reverently bent to the ground while the
Lord was speaking to him. But now it struck him as funny that a
hundred-year old man could beget a child, and that Sarah could
give birth at the age of ninety! All he said to the Lord, however,
was, "Ah, that Ishmael may live in your presence!" (Gn 17:18).
The Lord then said:

Sarah your wife is to bear you a son,
And him you shall call by the name of Isaac,
(A name that connotes either smiles or laughter,
As if this were a joke that God, too, enjoyed).
With him and his offspring after him
My Covenant will be established for ever.

I have heard your prayer for Ishmael;
I will bless him and make him notably fertile:
The father of twelve chieftains will he become,
And I will make a great nation of him.
But my Covenant will be maintained through Isaac,
Whom Sarah will bear you next year at this time. (Gn 17:19–21)

Then the Lord went up from Abraham. That same day the Patriarch circumcised himself, his thirteen-year old son Ishmael, and every other male in his household, all in accord with what God had ordered.

Not long afterward God appeared to the Patriarch in the Valley of Mamre. Abraham was sitting at the entrance flap of his tent during the hottest part of the day when he saw three men nearby. He found out later that one of them was the Lord, while the other two were angels. The Patriarch ran to meet them and made a profound salaam, saying, "I beg you, sir, if I may ask this favor, please do not go on past your servant. Let some water be brought, so that you may bathe your feet and then recline in the shade of this tree. And before you go on, let me bring you a little food, and then you may pass on your way." They replied, "You may do as you have suggested." Abraham quickly went to the tent to find Sarah. "Hurry," he told her, "take three measures of fine flour and knead it into loaves of bread!" Then, running out to the herd, he selected a prime calf which he gave to his herdsman to prepare. Finally, taking butter, milk, and the cooked veal, he laid this repast before his guests and stood waiting under the tree while they ate.

After they had eaten, the guests inquired, "Where is your wife Sarah?" "There in the tent," he replied. Then one of them remarked, "I will return to you without fail about this time next year. By then your wife will have a son." Sarah was listening near the entrance of the tent, and at this point she quietly laughed, aware that she and her husband were both advanced in years and that her menstrual periods had ceased long ago. The Lord then addressed Abraham, "Why did Sarah laugh and say, 'Am I really going to have a baby, despite my being an old woman?' After all, is anything too wonderful for El Shaddai to do? At the appointed time, about this time next year, I will return to you, and Sarah will have a son." Sarah became afraid and denied that she had laughed. But God rejoined, "Yes, laugh you did" (Gn 18:1–15).

Sodom and Gomorrah

With Abraham accompanying them as a guide, the three heavenly guests left and descended the precipitous slopes to the southeast until they were within sight of Sodom. Here the Lord waited while his angels went on into the city. The Patriarch entreated the Lord not to destroy the town as long as there could be found even as few as fifty righteous men within it—or forty—or thirty—or twenty—or even ten. And God heard his prayer. The Lord then departed from Abraham, and Abraham returned home.

When the two angels reached Sodom that evening, they came upon Lot sitting at the town gate. As soon as he saw them, Lot rose, bowed deeply, and invited them to come to his house and stay the night. During the night a rabble of men surrounded the house, intending to abuse Lot's guests. Lot went outside and attempted to placate them by offering them his two virgin daughters instead.* When they insisted, and threatened Lot with the same fate as his guests, the angels pulled him inside the house and bolted the door. As the gang started to advance on the door, the angels struck the attackers blind. The angels then informed Lot that God was going to destroy the town, and that he and his family should flee in order to escape annihilation. At dawn the angels led Lot, his wife, and two daughters out of Sodom and told them to run for their lives, neither stopping nor looking back. Lot gained a settlement above the plain just as God rained down fire and brimstone on Sodom and Gomorrah, turning the whole valley into a scene of billowing smoke. Lot's wife looked back, and was changed into a column of salt.

That a catastrophe befell the Dead Sea area at some geologically and archaeologically undesignated time, there is no doubt. There is evidence that a violent earthquake occurred which was accompanied by subterranean explosions and showers of bituminous

---

*The unnatural vice of sodomy derives its name from this incident. The Israelites held it an abomination, punishable by death (Lv 18:22; 20:13). It was, however, common practice among the neighboring nations.

fragments and perhaps also by a great conflagration of natural gas. But we have no proof that this was God's punishment of Sodom and Gomorrah.

After these events, Abraham migrated to the Negeb, settling in the lowland at the edge of the wilderness of Shur. He established temporary headquarters at Gerar in the land of the Amalekite king, Abimelech. As they had done in Egypt long before, Abraham and Sarah dissembled their relationship as husband and wife, saying simply that they were brother and sister. Even though she was now an old woman, Sarah was taken by Abimelech into his tent at night. But God intervened and rendered Abimelech and his harem impotent. As soon as Abimelech realized the cause of his misfortune, he restored Sarah to Abraham, and gave Abraham a thousand pieces of silver, along with some sheep, cattle, and slaves. Abraham then interceded with God for the curse on Abimelech to be lifted, and it was lifted.

CHAPTER TWO

ISAAC

Genesis 21—36; 1 Chronicles 1:34—54

Abraham's Faith Is Tested

As he had promised, the Lord saw to it that Sarah now conceived a son. It may have been about 1910 B.C. when she gave birth to Isaac—the one through whom the promise of the Covenant was to endure. On the day of the boy's circumcision, Sarah rejoiced, laughing for joy at God's faithfulness. Later, on the day that Isaac was weaned, Abraham presided over a great festive meal. But Sarah insisted that Hagar and her son Ishmael be driven out of the camp so as not to endanger Isaac's inheritance. Abraham dolefully assented, consoled by God's promise to make a great nation of Ishmael. Ishmael eventually became a desert bowman and through Hagar's intervention acquired an Egyptian wife.

The Amalekite chieftain, Abimelech, and the commander of his troops came to Abraham and entered into a formal pact with him at a place called Beersheba. The man of faith planted a tamarisk tree in commemoration and invoked the name of the everlasting God. Abraham and his household remained there in the Negeb for a long time.

Some years later, the Lord put Abraham's faith to a supreme test. God told him:

Now take your son, your truest child Isaac,
To whom you are bound by ties of love,
And go with him to the land of Moriah.
There you shall make me a holocaust
Of him on a hilltop I will show you. (Gn 22:2)

Abraham roused Isaac and two of his servants before dawn the next morning. Abraham chopped and bundled the wood for the sacrifice, and they left. On the third day, Abraham looked up and saw from afar the place the Lord had designated for the holocaust. He said to his servants, "Stay here with the donkey; the boy and I are going on up there to perform an act of worship and will come back to you here." He loaded the kindling on Isaac's back and carried the knife and the firestone in his own hands. Puzzled, Isaac asked, "Father, the wood and the firestone are on hand, but where is the lamb for a burnt offering?" "My son," replied Abraham, "the Lord himself is going to provide the sacrificial lamb" (Gn 22:7–8).

At the appointed site (tradition locates it on one of the two hills of the future Jerusalem), the Patriarch built an altar and piled his wood on top of it. He bound Isaac and laid him on the heap of faggots, stretched out his hand, and clasped the knife to slay his son. But an angel of God called from heaven, "Abraham, Abraham, do not raise your hand to the boy. Do not do him harm! Now I know you are devoted to God, since you have not withheld your only true son from me" (Gn 22:11–12). Abraham then saw a ram that was snagged by its horns in a bramble bush. He took the ram and offered it as a holocaust in place of Isaac. The angel called again to him:

The Lord God declares,
"By my own self I swear,
Seeing you have not denied
Your only true son to me,
I will shower you with blessings,
Making those who descend from you
As many as the stars of heaven
And as many as the grains of sand

On the seashore. Your progeny
Will possess the gates of their foes.
All the nations on earth will be blessed
Through them, because you obeyed me." (Gn 22:16–18)

Then Abraham and Isaac rejoined the servants and the four of
them traveled together toward their Beersheba home.

Later, while they were at Hebron, Sarah died at the age of 127.
Abraham traveled a few miles northward and visited his Hittite
neighbors in order to negotiate the purchase of a burial plot. He
obtained the field of Machpelah, which was situated near Mamre,
for the price of 400 silver shekels. There Abraham buried Sarah in
a cave.

Rebekah Becomes Isaac's Wife

When Isaac neared forty years of age Abraham decided that it
was time to find a wife for his son. Moreover, he wanted Isaac to
marry from among his kinsfolk, rather than from among the Canaanites. So he summoned the Damascene bondsman Eliezer, his
steward, and instructed him to go to the region of Haran to find
Isaac a wife among his relatives there. The steward, having sworn
his obedience to Abraham and been assured that an angel would
go before him, was sent off with ten camels and a variety of fine
gifts. It was near evening when he reached the well at the outskirts
of the settlement of Nahor. He prayed that God would guide him
in a specific way: that of the young women who came to the well
that evening to draw water the one whom the Lord had selected
to be Isaac's wife would not only give Eliezer a drink of water
when he asked her for it, but would also offer to draw water for
his camels.

As Eliezer's camels knelt at the trough, a beautiful young virgin
named Rebekah came to the well with a pitcher on her shoulder.
When she had filled her pitcher Eliezer said to her, "Please tilt your
pitcher and let me have a drink." She lowered the vessel on her
arm so that he could drink from it, and at the same time remarked,
"I'll draw water for your camels too, until they've had enough"

(Gn 24:18–19). After the camels had been taken care of, Eliezer presented her with gifts—a gold ring weighing half a shekel and a pair of gold bracelets weighing ten shekels. He then asked her whose daughter she was and inquired whether there was room at her father's house for him to spend the night. He discovered that she was the daughter of Bethuel, son of Nahor, and thus a grandniece of Abraham. She also said that there was enough straw and fodder for the animals, as well as room for Eliezer to lodge.

This Hebrew Aramaean family extended a hearty welcome to Eliezer as to one blessed by God, and water was brought for the washing of feet. But Eliezer, who had bowed down in worshipful thanksgiving to Abraham's God, would not recline to eat until he had first explained his mission. He said that his master Abraham was a very rich man, possessing flocks and herds, silver and gold, male and female slaves, and camels and donkeys. Eliezer then explained how he had been sent by Abraham to choose a wife from among his master's kinsmen for Abraham's son, Isaac. After Bethuel and Laban (Rebekah's brother) agreed that it was God's will for Rebekah to marry Isaac, Eliezer lavished upon the future bride ornaments of gold and silver. The steward desired to depart with her the next morning, but Rebekah's mother and brother begged him to delay for another ten days. Rebekah, however, announced that she was ready to leave at once. Accompanied by her nurse, she joined Eliezer's company and set off for Canaan.

Isaac was walking one evening in the fields nearby the well of Lahai Roi when he saw the group approaching. Upon learning that the figure in the field was Isaac, Rebekah quickly veiled her face and alighted from her camel. Isaac took Rebekah into his tent and made her his wife.

Abraham remarried and of his new wife, Keturah, he fathered six more sons. He kept them apart from Isaac and the promised inheritance. At their maturity he sent them away to the east, where with the descendants of Ishmael they gave rise to some of the roving tribes of Arabia. Then, at about 1835 B.C., a century after God's command to him to go forth from Haran, the Patriarch died at 175 years of age. Isaac and Ishmael buried him alongside Sarah in the cave of Machpelah, which came to be known as the tomb of the Patriarchs.

CHAPTER THREE

JACOB

Genesis 25:20—50:14; 1 Chronicles 2:1–2

Esau and Jacob

For twenty years of her married life Rebekah proved to be barren, but about 1850 B.C., when Isaac was about sixty, she finally conceived and gave birth to twin boys. Esau, the first to be born, was a woolly, red-haired baby who grew up to be a skillful hunter. Jacob, a little slower issuing from the womb, became a man who quietly tended his father's fields and herds. Isaac prized the lusty, willful Esau more, whereas Rebekah favored the retiring, cautious Jacob.

One day, when Jacob had cooked a tempting reddish-colored broth, thickened with lentils and morsels of bread, Esau flung himself into the tent deathly tired and famished. Esau craved the soup so much that the crafty Jacob offered it to him in exchange for his birthright as the elder son. Esau scornfully complied and sold his birthright to his brother for the bread-thickened soup. This transaction was to be fraught with momentous consequences: Esau married Hittite women, and his descendants were to be the Edomites; Jacob married Hebrew women, and from him were to descend the Israelites, the people of God.

The Patriarch Isaac raised animals, but also grew crops. He became so prosperous that Abimelech, the Amalekite ruler, judged

that Isaac had become a threat to him and pressed him to move
his encampment away. Isaac did so and relocated in another dis-
trict of the valley of Gerar. He found his father's wells spitefully
filled and destroyed. He redug those wells. But because of disputes
between his shepherds and those of Abimelech's people as to
whom the rights of certain wells belonged, he moved his camp
again, this time to Beersheba. There he built an altar and
invoked the name of the Lord God, who had appeared to him
again and said:

> I am your father Abraham's God.
> No need to fear, since I am with you.
> I will bless you and make your descendants many
> For the sake of my servant Abraham. (Gn 26:24)

Abimelech came over to Isaac from Gerar with the captain of his
troops, just as he had come to Abraham years before, to draw up
a pact. Isaac agreed, and a feast was held in commemoration.

As the peaceful years passed at Beersheba, Isaac began to lose
his sight. Although, in fact, he was to live twenty more years, Isaac
felt that he might die shortly and declared that the time had
arrived for him to give his last blessing. He called to Esau to shoot
some game with his bow, and then make "an appetizing dish for
me, such as I like, and bring it to me to eat, so that I may give you
my special blessing before I die" (Gn 27:4). Such a blessing would
carry with it the Patriarch's legacy.

On hearing this, Rebekah and Jacob resolved to trick Esau out
of the inheritance. Rebekah told Jacob to go and choose a pair of
choice kids from the flock. Then she would concoct the kind of
appetizing dish her husband liked so well. "You shall take it to
your father, so that he may eat it and bless you before he dies."
Jacob trembled at the thought. "Esau is hairy, while my skin is
smooth. Should he touch me he will know, and he will curse me
instead." His mother replied, "Let his curse fall on me in that case"
(Gn 27:10–13). Then she dressed Jacob in some of Esau's clothes,
and having covered the smoothness of his neck and forearms with
the kids' pelts, she thrust the savory into his hands along with
some bread.

"Father," Jacob said, "I am Esau your first born. I have done as you wished. Please sit up and eat some of my game, so that you may give me your special blessing." "How did you succeed so quickly, my son?" asked Isaac. "It was God's will I came across what I hunted as soon as I did," answered Jacob. "Then come closer, son," the old man said, "that I may feel you, to learn whether you really are my son Esau or not"—Jacob drew near his father, so that he could touch him—"for the voice is Jacob's, yet the forearms are Esau's." He persisted, "Are you really my son Esau?" "Yes," Jacob lied again. "Then serve me your game, son, that I may eat of it and then give you my blessing." Isaac ate, and drank wine. Then he said, "Come closer, son, and kiss me" (Gn 27:19–27). Jacob drew close and kissed his father.

As soon as the Patriarch caught the smell of Jacob's clothing, he blessed him, saying:

Ah, the smell of my son is the smell of a laden field blessed by the Lord! God give you dew from heaven and wealth from the earth, with an abundance of grain and wine! May peoples serve you, nations pay you homage! Be the master of your brothers, and let the sons of your mother bow down to you! (Gn 27:27–29)

At that moment Esau returned and prepared the tasty dish his father had requested. As he presented his father with it, the aged Isaac learned that he had been deceived. Esau's cry was loud and bitter. "Father, have you no blessing left for me?" "I appointed him your master," Isaac moaned, "gave him his brothers for his servants, supplied the grain and the wine to him." When Esau pleaded, "Father, please give me a blessing, too," Isaac remained silent. At this Esau burst into tears (Gn 27:36–38). He hated his brother Jacob now and threatened to kill him. Rebekah told Jacob to flee to her brother Laban in Haran. Before Jacob left, Isaac gave him a blessing and commanded him to take a wife from among Laban's daughters, since they were of Hebrew Aramaean blood.

On what was probably the first leg of his journey, Jacob came to Luz. Since night was falling, he decided to sleep there, his head

cushioned on a stone. While he slept, he dreamed of a stairs that
reached up to heaven upon which angels passed up and down. The
Lord was leaning over him, repeating the promise made to Jacob's
father and grandfather. The Lord also said, "I will protect you
wherever you may go" (Gn 28:15). In the morning Jacob made his
pillow-stone a monument and poured oil over it. And he changed
the name of the place to Bethel, which means "house of God," and
promised a tithe of his income to the Lord in return for a safe
journey.

Jacob's Years at Haran

When Jacob reached the Haran countryside, he met a shepherd-
ess named Rachel, who was one of Laban's daughters. He fell in
love with her and kissed her. Although Rachel was a beautiful
woman, her elder sister Leah was unattractive. Their father, Rebekah's brother and therefore Jacob's uncle, dealt slyly with his
nephew. Both Laban and Rebekah, brother and sister, were given
to deceitfulness. In order to have Rachel for his wife, Jacob agreed
to work for his uncle for a period of seven years. When the seven
years were over, the family held a celebration. But following the
festivity, wily Laban put his daughter Leah—instead of Rachel—
to bed with the befuddled Jacob, who did not discover the trick
until morning. Leah was now Jacob's wife. Jacob, nevertheless, still
desired Rachel so much that he put aside his anger and agreed to
serve an additional seven years as Laban's shepherd in order to
marry her.

Eleven sons were born to Jacob during those many years of
travail at Haran. Leah first bore Reuben, then Simeon, Levi, and
Judah. Rachel, who was barren, gave her slave-girl, Bilhah, to
Jacob as a wife; Bilhah gave birth to Dan and Naphtali. At one
point, when Leah also became unable to conceive children, she
gave Jacob her slave-girl, Zilpah, who bore him Gad and Asher.
When young Reuben happened to find some mandrakes in a field,
Rachel desired them so much that she allowed Leah to sleep with
Jacob in return for them. Leah then conceived Issachar and Zebu-
lon. Later, God opened Rachel's womb for the first time, and she
brought forth Jacob's eleventh son, Joseph.

As the years passed, Jacob looked forward to his release from serfdom. He wanted to provide for the future of his household, and probably for this reason volunteered to remain with Laban six years further while he built up his flocks. Jacob proposed to Laban that he receive as wages whatever dark sheep and spotted goats appeared among his father-in-law's flocks during those six years. Laban agreed, and they separated the animals into distinct groups according to color. In the Middle East sheep flocks were almost uniformly light in color, goat flocks uniformly dark; the animals that were different were undesirable oddities. From that time on, any off-colored sheep or goat that appeared in the flocks tended by Jacob was to belong to him.

To heighten the likelihood of such births Jacob resorted to a stratagem. The animals often mated near the watercourses where they came to drink. Jacob peeled back some of the bark from the young branches of almond, plane, and poplar trees that he found. He put these in the runnels so that the animals would see them as they drank. His thinking was that when the animals mated the sight of the variegated branches would stimulate them to produce mottled offspring. But Jacob also followed a careful breeding program for his sheep in particular: He allowed them to mate only among the dark-colored stock. Furthermore, with the practiced eye of a shepherd he let only the stronger of Laban's pure-colored white animals breed with his vari-colored animals, thus strengthening his own flocks at the expense of his father-in-law. In time, animals once considered blemished and flawed thus became a thoroughbred strain of *Ovis* and *Capra*. As these flocks of his multiplied, Jacob grew very prosperous.

Jacob's Return to Canaan

Laban and his sons became resentful as they saw Jacob increase in wealth. The Lord spoke to Jacob and told him to return to his homeland. Jacob discussed the matter with his wives, recounting to them how long and hard he had worked for their father and how many times he had been duped by him. But God had blessed him in spite of that, to the point where his flocks were larger and

more healthy than those of Laban. Jacob then told them how the
Lord had spoken to him through an angel, saying:

I am the God of Bethel,
Where you poured oil on a stone
And made a vow to me.
Up, then, and leave this country!
Return to the land of your birth. (Gn 31:13)

Rachel and Leah not only agreed with what Jacob said, but expressed bitterness toward their father for his stinginess in not
giving back to them their dowries, which were the shares of their
inheritance.

So Jacob and his family quickly prepared to return to "God's
kinsman," Isaac, and to the land of Canaan. Without betraying
their intentions, they mounted their camels and quietly departed,
driving their livestock before them. At that time Laban was away
shearing sheep.

Jacob and his party had forded the upper Euphrates and traveled as far as Mount Gilead, a long distance away, in the seven
days that passed before Laban was able to catch up with them.
Laban complained loudly about the stealth of Jacob's departure,
about his daughters being taken from him like captives, and about
Jacob's foolishness in foregoing the festivities that would, he said,
have accompanied their leave-taking. "And why," Laban asked,
"did you take away my household gods?" (Gn 31:30). Unknown
to Jacob, Rachel had made away with these. Jacob naturally dis-
claimed the theft and allowed Laban to search his tents. Rachel
had hidden the idols in her camel's litter. She pretended to be
suffering a difficult menstruation, and would not rise from where
she was sitting on top of the litter, thus preventing Laban from
rummaging through it. In this affair, she was indeed her father's
daughter.

At this point Jacob lost his temper and upbraided Laban for his
demeaning search. He reminded Laban of his twenty years of
faithful service, and of the fact that he had received nothing but
hard, even unjust treatment from him in return. After all that,
Jacob said, Laban would have sent him away empty-handed. The

Lord warned Laban in a dream not to do Jacob any harm, so the two men ended the affair by making a pact. Jacob and Laban set up a cairn at Gilead to seal their agreement, and they parted in peace.

In order to return to the land of Canaan, Jacob and his household had to pass through a land where they were within reach of Esau, Jacob's brother, whose domain was Edom and the mountains of Seir. To learn if Esau still burned with hatred for him, Jacob sent couriers ahead to inform his brother of his great material prosperity and to win his brother's favor.

The embassy seemed to have failed. The couriers returned with the ominous news that Esau had set out toward Jacob at the head of a contingent of 400 men. Immediately Jacob divided his group into two separate sections so that if one were attacked, the other could escape. Then Jacob turned to God. When he reached the Jabbok River at about ten miles from the point where it flows into the Jordan, he prayed that he might be delivered from an attack by his brother. Jacob said to God that he had only his shepherd's staff when he crossed the Jordan twenty years before, while now, returning to Canaan at the divine command, he had grown to such an extent that he could divide his household into two companies. He beseeched God to save them and reminded him of the promise that he had inherited from his grandfather Abraham.

Jacob sent his families ahead, while he himself remained at a place he named Peniel, staying there to pray. During the night an angel came and wrestled with him. The angel was unable to best Jacob, but at daybreak he struck Jacob on the hip, laming him for life. Jacob forced the angel to bless him, however, and in so doing the angel conferred a new name upon him—Israel. Hence it was that his descendants would be known as Israelites.

When Jacob first found out that Esau was advancing upon him, he picked from among his flocks a large, impressive gift to present to his brother in the hope of mollifying his anger. The gift consisted of 200 female and twenty male goats, 200 ewe and twenty ram sheep, thirty camels in milk with their calves, forty cows and ten bulls, twenty she-asses and ten donkeys.

In the end, Jacob's fears proved unfounded. At a spot about twenty-eight miles north of the Dead Sea, Esau came up and embraced his brother with tears of reconciliation. At first Esau refused the presents, but when pressed, he accepted them. He then volunteered to lead the way for the train. Jacob, perhaps not fully trusting his brother's intentions, refused Esau's offer, preferring to make his own way into Canaan.

On the Way to Hebron

The limping Patriarch Jacob-Israel turned his traveling throng toward the western highland. After resting at Succoth they crossed the Jordan and eventually encamped on the narrow valley floor across from the Hivite settlement of Shechem. Perhaps the Patriarch had entertained some thought of remaining there, for he bought the land that he was occupying for one hundred silver shekels from Hamor, ruler of that territory. If so, the bloody affair that soon occurred was to change his mind.

Dinah, the daughter of Jacob by Leah, was raped by Shechem, the son of Hamor. After committing this deed, Shechem burned to have Dinah in marriage. Hamor courteously visited Jacob-Israel in order to propose this marriage and also an alliance of their two peoples by this and future intermarriages. But Dinah's brothers, thirsting to revenge their sister's rape, slyly opposed the marriage on the basis of the fact that Hamor and his people were uncircumcised. Hamor and Shechem convinced all the able-bodied men of their community to be circumcised along with themselves.

Three days later, when the newly circumcised men were still in serious pain and, consequently, disabled, Jacob's sons Simeon and Levi took their revenge. They entered the village, put every male to the sword, looted the houses, captured the women and children, and took away the sheep, cattle, and donkeys. The Patriarch objected to his sons' handiwork and declared that their deed was bound to arouse the hatred of the surrounding peoples. Simeon and Levi only rejoined, "Should our sister have been treated like a harlot?" (Gn 34:31).

God told Jacob-Israel to move on, make camp at Bethel, and build him an altar there. The Patriarch ordered his people to do away with whatever idols they possessed and to wash themselves and don fresh garments—all as an act of purification and thanks-giving to God, who had delivered them from danger. This they did, and Jacob-Israel took all the fetishes and charms and even earrings, and buried them under an oak tree. The Israelites then broke camp and continued on their journey, unharassed by the native peoples.

When they arrived at Bethel, Jacob-Israel erected an altar to God as he had been commanded. Then the Patriarch set up a stone marker on which a libation was made and oil poured. God spoke to him again:

You whose name is Jacob
Are now to be called Israel.
Almighty God am I.
Be fruitful and multiply.
A nation, indeed an assembly
Of nations, shall stem from you,
And kings issue from your loins.
The land that once I gave
To Abraham and to Isaac,
This land I now give to you. (Gn 35:10–12)

They moved on from Bethel toward Hebron. Along the way Rachel died in giving birth to the Patriarch's last son, Benjamin. She was buried at Bethlehem, with a gravestone set up to mark her place of rest. Farther up the highland road, at Migdal-eder, the Patriarch was distressed to learn that his eldest son, Reuben, had committed incest by having lain with Bilhah, Rachel's slave-girl and the mother of Dan and Naphtali.

Jacob-Israel reached his father's side at Hebron after more than twenty years of absence. It was that long since Isaac had been beguiled into imparting his final blessing to Jacob. Blind old Isaac at his death, probably in about 1703 B.C., was 180 years of age. Israel and Esau buried him at Mamre, alongside their grandparents Abraham and Sarah.

CHAPTER FOUR

JOSEPH

Genesis 37—50; 1 Chronicles 2:1–2

The Fancy Coat

Israel settled down at last in the land of Canaan with his twelve sons about him. The Patriarch doted on Joseph, Rachel's first born, and when the lad was seventeen, Israel gave him a long, fine-woven coat as a token of his great affection. This roused envy in his other sons, and their envy soon gave way to anger. Their dislike of him grew so strong that they would hardly speak to him. To make matters worse, Joseph reported to his father certain offenses committed by Gad, Asher, Dan, and Naphtali, his half-brothers by Bilhah and Zilpah.

The fraternal hatred came to a boil when Joseph bragged of some dreams he had had. In one dream all his brothers were binding grain into sheaves; Joseph's sheaf rose up and theirs all bowed down low before it. In another dream the sun and moon (representing his father and mother) and eleven stars (representing his brothers) all bowed down to him. On hearing of these visions, the Patriarch observed the jealousy of the brothers and he reproved Joseph. But he himself pondered what the meaning of those dreams might be.

One day, when the brothers were grazing their flocks in the pastures at Shechem, the Patriarch sent Joseph there to bring back news of them to him. Joseph trudged the fifty-mile distance from Hebron to the Shechem valley. He hunted high and low for his brothers and wandered about everywhere in the area. A man informed him that they had moved to Dothan, fourteen miles farther north.

At Dothan the brothers caught sight of the fancy long coat of Joseph as he was coming toward them in the distance, and they hatched a plot to kill the lad when he came up to them. They decided to throw his dead body into a pit and then spread the story that wild beasts had mauled and eaten him. Reuben, the oldest of the brothers and their foreman, was directly responsible to the Patriarch and hoped to preserve the boy's life for his father's sake. He therefore cautioned them not to shed a drop of Joseph's blood, but rather to cast him into a dry cistern that was there and leave him still alive.

What actually took place was this. When the advancing youth had drawn up with his brothers, they tore the fancy long coat off his back, tossed him into the empty well, and sat down to eat and talk things over. As they sat there, a caravan approached from the direction of Gilead and the Jabbok valley, its camels laden with gum, balm, and resin. Judah, the ringleader of the dissident brothers, proposed that they sell Joseph to the caravan instead of reddening their hands with his blood. The brothers agreed, hauled Joseph up, and sold him for twenty pieces of silver. The captive Joseph passed into the possession of some Midianite merchants who carried him away to the auction block in Egypt.

Reuben, apparently not present when this transaction was taking place, went back to the pit expecting to rescue his younger brother. When he peered in and saw that the boy's body had disappeared, he tore his clothes in anguish. Then the brothers took the fine-woven long coat, spattered it with the blood of a goat, and sent it to their father with the inquiry, "Could this be Joseph's coat?" Old Israel moaned, "This is the coat I gave my son; the claws and the jaws of wild beasts have done for him!" (Gn 37:33). He rent his garments, donned sackcloth, and mourned unceasingly. His sons and daughters gathered to comfort him in vain, for he kept saying weepingly, "I will go down mourning to my son in the nether world" (Gn 37:35).

Joseph's Early Days in Egypt

The caravaneers, meanwhile, had put Joseph on the block in the slave market at Memphis, where he was bought by a man named Potiphar, captain of the Pharaoh's guard. Potiphar was pleased with Joseph's competence and made the young man his steward, giving him charge of his entire estate, house and all. With God's blessing, everything went so smoothly that the captain found he needed to give personal attention only to his meal times.

Joseph was a handsome young fellow—keen, polished, well-built—and Potiphar's wife determined to seduce him. She boldly invited him to lie with her; again and again she tempted him. But Joseph, slave though he was, refused to comply with her desires. The master had put him in charge, and the master's wife was untouchable. "Besides," he said, "how could I do so great a wrong? It would be a sin against my God" (Gn 39:9).

But one day, when Joseph's duties called him inside the house, she accosted him. She clutched him by his cloak and demanded that he sleep with her. Joseph tore himself away abruptly, leaving his cloak in her hands, and fled outdoors. When Potiphar came home, the spurned woman complained bitterly about Joseph's insolence. "The Hebrew slave whom you brought here broke in on me, to make sport of me. But when I screamed for help, he left his cloak beside me and fled outside" (Gn 39:17–18). The captain was furious. He took the cloak as proof of Joseph's guilt and clapped him in the royal prison.

For some years the maligned young man languished among the Pharaoh's prisoners. But God moved the heart of the chief jailer to trust Joseph; he eventually made Joseph his deputy and put him in charge of all the other prisoners.

Now it happened that the Pharaoh's head cupbearer and head baker had both been imprisoned and were suffering from depression. Each had had a dream that was unintelligible to everyone except Joseph, who was able to interpret their dreams for them. The cupbearer's dream, he said, meant that he would be released from prison in three days and regain his high position. But the baker's dream signified that in three days he would be put to death. And indeed on the third day, which was the day of the

Pharaoh's birthday celebration, the cupbearer was restored to his place of honor and the baker was executed as Joseph had predicted.

Several years later, when Joseph was thirty years old, the Pharaoh had a frightening twofold dream that none of his fortunetellers or sages were able to fathom. The cupbearer remembered the man he had met in jail who had so brilliantly interpreted his and the chief baker's dreams, and he told the Pharaoh about him. The Pharaoh immediately commanded Joseph to be brought to him to expound the meaning of the royal dreams. The young Hebrew quickly shaved and changed clothes, and then presented himself before the king, his cabinet, and the royal court. As the Pharaoh told of his double dream Joseph said to him, "It is not I, but God, who will give the Pharaoh the right answer" (Gn 41:16).

The Pharaoh had dreamed he was standing on the bank of the Nile when seven cows, all shapely and fat, came up out of the water at the river's edge and began grazing on the grasses of the marsh. These were followed by seven other cows, all gaunt and misshapen creatures—such miserable specimens as had never been seen in all of Egypt. The sickly cows ate the healthy ones, but were none the better for their gorging on flesh: They were as lank, squalid, and sluggish as before. Then the dream changed. The Pharaoh saw seven cereal spears with plump grains growing in a single luxuriant clump, followed by seven scrawny, blighted blades with poor cereal heads. The poor grain swallowed up the good.

Joseph spoke out in explanation. The Pharaoh's dreams both came to the same thing: The fine-looking cattle and the splendid cereal grains stood for seven years of plenty, while the drought-blasted cereals and the emaciated cattle represented seven ensuing years of famine. In a word, Egypt was going to have seven years of magnificent fertility, followed by an equal number of years of want. Great indeed would be the time of fruitfulness, but just as great would be the subsequent famine, so great in fact that no one would remember the plenty they had previously enjoyed.

This dream had come to Pharaoh because the events it foretold were foreordained by the will of God. Because the events were soon to come about, Joseph advised the Pharaoh to choose a man known to be hard-working and wise to be governor of the whole of Egypt. He should also appoint provincial overseers who would levy a tax of a fifth part of all the land's produce during the seven years of abundance that lay ahead and then store up the grain in magazines. In this way food would be set aside within the towns and conserved until it would be needed.

Joseph Is Named Governor of Egypt

Pleased by Joseph's brilliant elucidation and solution, the Pharaoh and his cabinet of ministers saw no one on Egypt's broad horizon who so fully possessed the spirit of God as did this Hebrew slave. Admitting that he knew of no one as wise as Joseph, the Pharaoh immediately made him his viceroy, had him dressed in robes of finest linen, put a gold chain around his neck, and handed him the signet ring with the royal seal making him administrative head of the realm. He was to take precedence over all the nobles of the land, his chariot following none but the Pharaoh's chariot of state. Runners were to go before it crying, "Give way!" Henceforth, without Joseph's leave no man dared move hand or foot in all Egypt.

The Pharaoh then married him under the name of Zephenath-Paneah to the princess Asenath, daughter of the priest of the Sun-god Ra at Hierapolis. During the seven years of plenty, when Joseph was kept busy visiting all the provinces of the realm, Asenath bore him two sons. Joseph gave them the Hebrew names of Manasseh and Ephraim.

The seven years of plenty ended and famine began to stalk the land. When the people cried out for bread, the Pharaoh's terse reply was "Go to Joseph!" (Gn 45:51). Opening up the granaries, Joseph sold grain to all who dwelt in Egypt. But the famine spread from Egypt throughout the world at large, including the land of Canaan where Israel and the Israelites dwelt.

Hearing that there was grain for sale in Egypt, the Patriarch kept Benjamin at home with him and sent all his other sons to Egypt to buy grain. Since they were aliens in that land, the sons of Israel were referred to Joseph, and they bowed to the ground before him. Joseph recognized them as his brothers, but he spoke to them through an interpreter so that they would not know who he was. He was intent on giving them a hard time while he learned of the fortunes of the Hebrew clan. He accused them of being foreign spies, had them arrested, and grilled them about the Israelites himself. Through Reuben, speaking to him in the Aramaic tongue, he discovered that the eleven brothers were joined in regret over what they had done to a brother named Joseph. Through the interpreter, Joseph also made them tell him about Israel and Benjamin who had remained at home.

After keeping them in custody for three days, Joseph announced that he would let them have the food and go, provided they would come back to Egypt and show him they really had a younger brother Benjamin. He insisted, however, that one of them would have to be detained as surety for their word; so he took Simeon and bound him while they looked on. Then Joseph gave orders that the wicker baskets of their donkeys be filled and they be given provisions for their return journey. Unknown to his brothers he also commanded that the money they had paid be hidden within their feedsacks.

Back in Canaan the brothers told their father the whole bizarre story: how the strange, severe Egyptian lord had taken them for spies; how he was holding Simeon in bonds as their pledge to return with their remaining brother; and how they found the monies they had paid concealed in their feedsacks. The Patriarch refused to let them take Benjamin to Egypt with them, even though Reuben pledged the lives of his own sons for the boy's safety. Israel was adamant—Benjamin was not to be taken from him.

When the famine worsened and the grain brought from Egypt was exhausted, the Patriarch wanted his sons to go to Egypt again to buy food. But they would not go without Benjamin, for the Egyptian lord had made it clear that they would not be admitted to his presence unless their other brother came with them. "Why did you tell him there was another brother at home?" Israel demanded (Gn 43:6). The Egyptian lord had kept questioning them about their family—whether their father was still living, whether they had any other brothers. How could they have guessed that the lord would demand that Benjamin be brought to Egypt?

Israel's white head bowed in grief. If the Patriarch wanted to save the whole Hebrew clan from starvation, he would have to give in. Judah pledged Benjamin's safety, and Benjamin was allowed to leave. But to win the lord's favor, they were to take him a present of balm and honey, gum, resin, pistachio nuts and almonds, and were to refund him twice the amount of money found in the feedsacks.

Once more in Egypt, the sons of Israel came before the viceroy. Aware that Benjamin was with them, Joseph had his steward conduct the brothers to his home and told him to have a meat dish prepared for the midday dinner, which he said he would take together with them. The brothers, fearing that they were on the verge of being enslaved, detained the steward just outside the house and endeavored to explain the awkward matter of finding the payment money in their sacks on their way home from the first trip. The steward told them to rest easy: It must have been their God who had hidden the coins there. With that he brought Simeon to join them, ushered them all inside, offered them water for washing their feet, and went out again to see that their animals were given fodder. The brothers were finally convinced that, no matter how peculiar it seemed, they would be dining with the Egyptian lord. They readied their gifts, and when he arrived at noon handed them to him, prostrating themselves in deference.

The viceroy returned their greetings kindly and inquired after their old father's health. Looking at Benjamin, Joseph asked if he was that youngest brother of whom they had spoken. Then saying to him, "May God be good to you, my boy!" (Gn 43:29), and finding himself close to tears, he excused himself, and went aside and wept in private. He bathed his face, collected himself, returned to the room, and ordered dinner to be served. Joseph ate apart from his guests, but had servings from his own dishes carried to Benjamin's plate until it was heaped up much higher than the others. Benjamin by now was a lad in his middle teens, about the age of Joseph when he was thrown into the well. Joseph himself was probably about thirty-seven. After the Israelites had eaten and drunk with the viceroy and were preparing to leave, Joseph had his steward see that their sacks were stuffed full of dry food. Again their money was clandestinely inserted in the sacks. In addition, he ordered that his own silver drinking cup, a precious vessel, be hidden in Benjamin's sack along with the lad's wheat money.

The sons of Israel departed at daybreak. They were just outside the city limits when the steward overtook them and charged them with stealing the prime minister's silver drinking cup. They denied the charge, not only disclaiming all knowledge of the crime but declaring that if the steward should find the cup in the belongings of any one of them, that man should die and the rest of the company be enslaved. The sacks were lifted to the ground for inspection; the cup was discovered in Benjamin's sack, and the brothers tore their clothes in anguished consternation.

After the donkeys were reloaded they were brought back to the viceroy's house with Judah at their head. Joseph chided them for abusing his hospitality by such folly, declaring that no one in all Egypt was as adept as he in reading omens in his drinking cup. All that the brothers could say in reply was that since this was God's doing, they were resigned to being made slaves. But the viceroy said, "No, only the man who had the cup in his possession is going to be enslaved; the rest of you are free to return safe and sound to your father" (Gn 44:17). Judah then asked if he might have a word in private with the viceroy. He told him that this younger brother was the only son left to their old father by his mother; there had been one other son by her, but he had been mauled and torn to pieces by wild beasts. If now deprived of this lad whom he loved so much, old Israel was certain to die. Judah said:

> I, your servant, got the boy from his father by going surety for him, saying, "If I fail to bring him back to you, father, you can hold it against me forever." Let me, your servant, therefore, remain in place of the boy as the slave of my lord, and let the boy go back with his brothers. (Gn 44:32–33)

At this, Joseph could no longer keep his feelings under control; he ordered his retainers to leave the room and bring the brothers back in. When they came he burst into tears, announcing that he, the viceroy, was their brother Joseph, the one whom they had sold into Egypt as a slave. So loudly did he weep that his servants heard him all through the house. The brothers did not know how to react to this; they were simply overwhelmed. But Joseph reassured them that he had forgiven them. He said it was not they, but God, who had sent him before them to live in Egypt, so that he could one day save their lives by supplying them food. It was God who made him the Pharaoh's viceroy, lord of his court and governor of all the land of Egypt.

Joseph rejoiced to hear that his father still lived. In the Pharaoh's name he issued an invitation for the Patriarch and his entire clan to come and live with him in Egypt. He told his brothers to go quickly back to their father and explain that his son Joseph was alive, and that God had made him the lord of all the land in Egypt. He now wished Israel to come and settle in the fertile land of Goshen in the Delta. There his children and his children's children would all be near the lord his son, and their cattle, flocks, and other possessions would all be secure against the five famine years still to come. They were to tell him that Joseph would see to it that Israel's House and its possessions did not perish from the earth. They were also to tell him of all the honors that Joseph enjoyed, and of the wonders they had seen in Egypt. "Hurry and bring my father down here" (Gn 45:13). Joseph wept and threw his arms around Benjamin, his full brother. After that they all dared to converse with him.

Israel and His House Come to Egypt

Joseph's servants carried the news of their master's loud weeping to the Pharaoh's palace, and the king and his court were pleased that Joseph's brothers had come to him. The king said to Joseph:

> Say to your brothers, "This is what you shall do: Load up your animals and go without delay to the land of Canaan. There get your father and your families, and then come back here to me; I will assign you the best land in Egypt, where you will live off the fat of the land." (Gn 45:17–18)

Then the king ordered wagons to transport Joseph's father with all haste. "Do not be concerned about your belongings, for the best in the whole land of Egypt shall be yours" (Gn 45:20). The Israelites were happy to comply. Joseph furnished them with wagons and provisions for the journey, gave Benjamin three hundred silver shekels and five sets of garments, and gave the others one garment apiece. To his father, Joseph sent ten stud donkeys laden with riches, and ten mare asses bearing wheat and bread for his father's journey to Egypt.

When they arrived in Canaan, the brothers reported all these events to Israel, who was so stunned by the news that at first he could not believe them. But at the sight of the wagons and provisions he came to accept that his son Joseph was really alive; and he said, "I must go and see him before I die" (Gn 45:23).

The Patriarch set forth for Egypt with his whole clan. The long train of people, wagons, and livestock made a stop at Beersheba, where Israel offered sacrifice to the God of his father Isaac. That night he had a vision in which God told him not to be anxious about going down to Egypt.

There I will make a great nation of you.
Not only will I go down with you
To Egypt; I will also bring you back here,
After Joseph shall have closed your eyes. (Gn 46:3–4)

So Israel's family of sons and grandsons, their women and their young—seventy people in all—arrived with their livestock in Egypt. Judah had gone on ahead, and Joseph rode his chariot over to Goshen to be on hand to greet his father. When they met he threw his arms around the Patriarch's neck and wept on his shoulder. Now that he had seen Joseph again, the old man pronounced himself ready to die.

Joseph, accompanied by five of his brothers, rode back to report to the Pharaoh his family's arrival at Goshen. He pointed out to the king that they were shepherds, a people whose way of life consisted of looking after herds and flocks of livestock. He presented his five brothers, and they asked the king's leave to stay in Goshen, a land they favored. Not only did the Pharaoh grant their request, despite the Egyptians' tendency to look askance at nomadic shepherds, but he even asked for capable men from among the Israelites to take charge of his own livestock. Afterward Joseph brought and presented his father to the king. Israel told the ruler that he was 130 years old—fewer and less happy years than those of his nomad fathers before him. The Patriarch then blessed the Pharaoh. At the king's direction, Joseph settled his father and his father's people on a holding in Egypt's best delta land, and he supplied them with food for their dependents. In the famine-ridden Egypt of that day, the position of the Israelites was truly enviable, and in Goshen their numbers multiplied.

The Patriarch was to live seventeen more years—to the age of 147—with his sight failing in those latter years. When death drew near he formally adopted Joseph's two sons, Manasseh and Ephraim, making them peers of Israel's sons and surrogates for their father in the future tribes. Israel kissed and embraced the boys, and then blessed them with the following prayer:

May God in whose ways my fathers Abraham and Isaac walked; may the God who has been my shepherd from my birth to this day; may the angel who has delivered me from all harm—bless these boys! May my name and the names of my fathers, Abraham and Isaac, live on in them! May they become teeming multitudes upon the earth! (Gn 48:15–16)

He then called all his sons together and imparted benedictions to them each in turn. Finally, Israel exacted an oath from Joseph to insure that he would be buried in Canann at Mamre, where his parents and grandparents, Abraham and Sarah, Isaac and Rebekah, and his wife Leah were entombed.

At the old man's death, Joseph threw himself upon Israel's body with tears and kisses. He then gave orders for the official undertakers in his service to embalm the body, a process that took forty days. The mourning of Egypt for Israel lasted seventy days. Joseph petitioned the king for permission to fittingly transport the Patriarch's remains to his last resting place in Canaan, and the Pharaoh agreed.

The great funeral cortege to Canaan formed a long procession.

It included Joseph and his family, plus all his brothers and their families. In fact, the whole Goshen settlement made the trip except for the children, who were left behind with the flocks and herds. Also in the retinue were nobles of the land of Egypt and dignitaries of the Pharaoh. Horsemen and chariots escorted the train.

The cortege followed the king's highway, the well-known and much-traveled route to the north through Edom and Moab. They stopped on a plain the Bible calls Goren-ha-atad, which lay beyond the Jordan. There they spent three days in lamentation. Then, fording the Jordan and passing on into the highland to Mamre and the cave of Machpelah, they desposited the sacred remains of Jacob-Israel in the ancestral tomb.

Upon their return to Egypt, the brothers were concerned that Joseph, now that his father was dead and buried, might wreak vengeance upon them for what they had done to him in his youth. Joseph learned of their fear and tearfully reassured them that he considered his kidnaping to have been God's will. His speech was in words of affection that touched and warmed their hearts.

When, in his old age, Joseph was about to die, he assured his relatives in the Goshen settlement that God would keep the Israelites in mind and surely bring them back, as he had sworn, to the Promised Land, the land of Abraham, Isaac, Jacob, and their descendants. And he made them swear that when this came about, they would bear the casket containing his embalmed body back to Canaan for burial.

The Chronology of the Patriarchal Period

The Patriarchal period opened with the arrival of Abraham in Canaan, and closed with the exit from Canaan and entry into Egypt of Jacob-Israel. These events were separated by 215 years. As has been seen, the date of 1935 B.C. for the period's start was arrived at from the best-supported biblical tradition. Using that date as an anchoring point of reference, we can determine other approximate, plausible dates in the Book of Genesis.

By this method it follows that Abraham would have been born in Ur in 2010 B.C., since he was 75 (Gn 12:4) upon entering Canaan in 1935 B.C. Ishmael's birth was in 1924 B.C., since at that time Abraham was 86 (Gn 16:16). The Covenant, the name changes, and the circumcising were in 1911 B.C., since Abraham was then 99 (Gn 17:24–25). The birth of Isaac was in 1910 B.C., when Abraham was 100 (Gn 21:5). The marriage of Isaac and Rebekah was in 1870 B.C., when Isaac was 40 (Gn 25:20). The twins Esau and Jacob were born in 1850 B.C., when Isaac was 60 (Gn 25:26). Abraham's death was in 1835 B.C., when he was 175 (Gn 25:7). The date of Jacob's entry into Egypt was 1720 B.C., when he was 130 (Gn 47:9). Jacob's death was in 1703 B.C., when he was 147 (Gn 47:48).

Joseph's chronology is somewhat more involved, since it rests upon a degree of supposition. The (first?) famine was already two years under way (Gn 45:6) when Joseph, having revealed his identity to his brothers, had them bring Israel and the Israelite community to live in Egypt (Gn 46:5–7, 26–27; 47:1). As stated above, the date of this event was quite likely 1720 B.C. At that time Joseph should have been about 39 years old, for he was 30 (Gn 41:46) when elevated to the rank of viceroy in what may well have been 1729 B.C. If we may assume that the seven years of plenty started at that time, then he was perhaps 37 when the era of famine began. Two years later he was reunited with his father and his Israelite relatives, who came to live in Goshen. His death at the age of 110 (Gn 50:26) would then have taken place at about 1649 B.C.

The chronology of Genesis places Jacob-Israel's lifetime at approximately 1850 B.C. to 1703 B.C. It is interesting to note the momentous historical occurrences that took place at opposite ends of the Fertile Crescent during his life. In the west, the Egyptian empire was overrun by the Hyksos, whose dominion over Egypt has been dated as beginning sometime prior to 1700 B.C. In the east, the Old Babylonian empire had the Code of Hammurabi imposed upon it by the celebrated conqueror and law-giver of that name, to whose reign archaeologists assign the approximate dates of 1728 B.C. to 1676 B.C. The Patriarch was contemporary to these world-shaping affairs.

CHAPTER FIVE

MOSES

Exodus; Leviticus; Numbers; Deuteronomy;
1 Chronicles 6:1–10

Centuries of Silence Intervene

The Pharaoh under whom Joseph served as viceroy was one of the Hyksos, the line of shepherd kings who ruled Egypt for a century and half during the fifteenth, sixteenth, and seventeenth dynasties between the middle and new Kingdoms. The Hyksos were a nomad Semitic people who had come out of the east sometime before 1700 B.C. They invaded and conquered Egypt, but absorbed Egyptian culture and adopted Egyptian names. They brought with them the wheel—on chariots, carts, wagons, etc.— and brought the horse to pull these vehicles.

The Hyksos kings were seated at Memphis, Avaris, and Heliopolis in the Delta, whence they ruled both lower and upper Egypt by means of strategically located garrisons. They were oppressive rulers, forcing the native princes of the old nobility whom they allowed to remain in power to pay them tribute. The throne also confiscated all lands and fields except those that formed adjuncts of the temples—a policy in which Joseph seems to have had a hand (Gn 47:13–22). Not surprisingly, the native governors struggled again and again to unseat their foreign masters. At length at Avaris the Hyksos were overthrown by Prince Ahmose of Thebes, the first Pharaoh of the eighteenth dynasty. Ahmose succeeded in expelling the aliens from Egypt. He pursued them as far as Palestine and destroyed the strongholds in which they took refuge.

The period in which the Hyksos reigned is the only era in Egypt's long history which left no memorials behind it. The reason was this: So bitter and fierce was the hatred in which the shepherd kings were held by the native population of Egypt that the memory of their dynasties was expunged from the papyri's hieroglyphic records. This lacuna, which once so perplexed students of Egyptology, was a deliberate attempt to consign the Hyksos to oblivion.

It was during this undocumented age that the Israelites came and settled in Goshen—likely in 1720 B.C., when Joseph was thirty-nine. With no papyri to shed light on those times, we have only an indication in the Bible that the first Israelites found happiness under Joseph's patronage and throve on the Delta's best grazing land. But the Bible then passes over in utter silence four successive so-called "generations" of the Hebrews. These generations as we now know were actually whole centuries, comprising from fourteen to sixteen generations as we now count them. During those hundreds of years the original seventy immigrant Israelite souls grew to a population of 600,000 persons. When the Bible takes up the story again, this large body of people was still living in Goshen, but with this difference: They were now living under oppression.

The People of God Suffer Oppression

When those four silent centuries had passed, the sons of Israel composed a populous settlement or cluster of settlements of unhappy people. The nineteenth dynasty of Pharaohs had grown uneasy over the presence of these twelve prolific non-native tribes. In the eyes of this warlike dynasty the Israelites were regarded as a threat to Egypt's security—as potential allies of the enemies of the state, the more dangerous because they lived inside the frontier of the Princes' Wall. Gradually the situation had degenerated from uneasiness to fear, and from fear to repression. When they were as yet still free, the Israelites might have pe-

titioned the king for permission to depart from Egypt; but they
had not done so, and for a time they continued to live in peace.

Sometime, however, probably during the twenty-year reign of
Seti I as Pharaoh (c.1319-c.1301 B.C.), the Egyptians took measures
to check the growth of this alien population. First, the midwives
of the Israelites were ordered to kill all new-born Israelite males.
When the midwives refused, the Pharaoh decreed that Hebrew
baby boys were to be drowned in the Nile.

Matters drew to a head under the reign of Rameses II (c.1301-
c.1234 B.C.). Rameses II was the tyrant who reigned during the
worst of the oppression of the Hebrews and was the Pharaoh
whom Moses confronted. While his predecessor, Seti I, had rebuilt
Avaris from its ruins, Rameses II inaugurated a program of massive
public works. To complete it he conscripted Hebrew men, using
them in forced labor gangs, in effect making them the nation's
slaves, From Exodus 1:11 we learn the Pharaoh employed them in
rebuilding and enlarging the store-cities of Pithom and Rameses,
supply points for the Princes' Wall. Under the whips of their
Egyptian overlords they labored in the brick-kilns, clay works,
and stone quarries, not to mention the drudgery of cartage and
hauling. Under this incessant toil and abuse, the Israelites groaned
to God for relief.

A boy born perhaps at the start of the reign of Seti I was to
deliver them. This baby's parents, Amram and Jochebed, were of
the tribe of Levi; the child had an older brother, Aaron, and a
sister. Under the law the infant had to be killed, but his mother
kept him hidden as long as she could. Finally, when he was three
months old, to preserve him from detection she put him in a
papyrus basket coated with bitumen and pitch to make it water-
tight, and she laid the basket among the bulrushes along the river's
edge. The boy's sister (likely Miriam) was stationed at a safe
distance to guard him.

Now it happened that the Pharaoh's daughter came down to the
river to bathe while her ladies-in-waiting walked along the bank
amid the rustling reeds and sedges. Spying the basket, the princess
ordered it brought to her. Inside she discovered a plaintively crying baby boy, and her heart went out to him. She knew at once
that it was a Hebrew infant; nevertheless, she resolved to take and

raise him as her foster child. The baby's sister, who had run up to the princess, volunteered to find a Hebrew woman to suckle the infant, and the princess said she would pay the wet-nurse. The girl went and called her mother. When the baby was weaned he was brought to the Pharaoh's daughter, by whom he was given the name of Moses. It was common practice among the Egyptians to append the enclitic *mose,* meaning born, to a given name, as in the case of the Pharaohs Ahmose and Thutmose.

Moses grew to manhood in the Pharaoh's palace. Presumably, he was trained in Egyptian art and science, yet was ever aware of his kinship with the Hebrew community. One day at the works, he saw an Egyptian taskmaster cruelly beating a Hebrew laborer. He killed the slave driver and, thinking there was no one else about, hid the body in the sand. The next day, however, upon returning to the same place, Moses found two Hebrews fighting with one another and tried to separate them. When he reproved the one in the wrong, the culprit asked him if he had set himself up as a prince and a judge and meant to kill him as the day before he had killed the Egyptian. Moses knew that his deed would soon become public knowledge and that the Pharaoh would issue a death-warrant for him. He fled across the Sinai Peninsula, eventually reaching Midian, just east of the Gulf of Aqaba.

One day, while sitting at the side of a well there, he saw some shepherds driving away seven young women who had come to water their father's flocks. Moses came to their defense, and watered the sheep himself. Reuel, a Midianite priest whom the Bible will later call Jethro, was the father of the seven sheep-tending girls. He was pleased when his daughters told him how the Egyptian had befriended them, and he offered the stranger his hospitality.

Moses made up his mind to stay with him. He settled there and married Zipporah, one of Reuel's daughters, who bore him two sons, Gershom and Eliezer. Thus during much of the terrible reign of Rameses II, Moses tranquilly tended his father-in-law's flocks, wandering from grazing plot to grazing plot as his remote forefathers had done.

And now God was to speak to Moses just as he had spoken to his ancestors. In Goshen the Israelites bewailed their abject slavery and besought God for help. The Lord God heard this plea and remembered the Covenant he had sworn with Abraham, Isaac, and Israel.

God's Call to Moses

Moses had driven his flocks down the Sinai Peninsula to Mount Horeb, known also as Mount Sinai. This was the mountain of God, so called because of the extraordinary thing that was about to happen there. Now, on the mountain, God appeared to Moses in the form of a flaming fire burning in the midst of a bramble bush. Moses saw the bush and approached in awe; though on fire the bush was not being consumed. As he came nearer God called to him from the flame:

> Come no closer! And take off your sandals,
> For the place where you stand is holy ground. (Ex 3:5)

At these words Moses covered his face, afraid to look on God.

> I am the God of your fathers, the God
> Of Abraham, Isaac, and Israel.
> I have witnessed the hardships of my people
> In Egypt, and have listened to their prayers to be saved
> From the slave drivers causing their sufferings.
> Well aware how badly they are abused,
> I have come down to rescue them
> From the Egyptians' hands, and lead them out
> Into a good and spacious land,
> A land that flows with milk and honey.
> Come now! I will send you to the Pharaoh
> To lead my people, the Israelites,
> Out of and from the land of Egypt. (Ex 3:6–8, 10)

Moses asked in reply, "Who am I that I should go to Pharaoh, and lead the Israelites out of Egypt?" (Ex 3:11). God answered:

I will be with you, and this is the proof
That it is I who am sending you:
When my people have been brought out of Egypt,
You will worship God on this very mountain. (Ex 3:12)

"But when I go to the Israelites and say to them, 'The God of
your fathers has sent me to you,' if they ask me, 'What is his
name?' what am I to tell them?" (Ex 3:13).

I Am Who Am. Yes, this is what
You are to tell the Israelites,
"It is I Am who has sent me to you."
You shall thus say to the Israelites,
"The God of your fathers has sent me to you,
The God of Abraham, Isaac, and Jacob.
Yahweh, your God, has sent me to you."
For Yahweh eternally is my name,
And by that title I shall be addressed
Throughout all future generations.
Go, assemble the Israelite elders and say,
"The Lord God of your fathers has appeared to me,
The God of Abraham, Isaac, and Jacob,
And he said, I have visited you and seen
The way you are being treated in Egypt.
So I will bring you out of the torment
Of Egypt and into the land where dwell
Canaanites, Hittites, and Amorites,
Perizzites, Hivites, and Jebusites,
A land that is flowing with milk and honey."
They will heed what you have to say to them.
Then with the elders of Israel
You will go to the Egyptian king and confront him,
Saying, "Yahweh, the God of the Hebrews,
Has called upon us. Permit us to go
A three-days' journey into the desert,
That we may offer sacrifice
To him who is the Lord our God."
Now I know that Egypt's king will not

Allow you to go, unless he is forced.
Then I will stretch out my hand, therefore,
And smite Egypt with all the prodigies
I hold in store for it. After that,
It is certain he will allow you to go.
And so high in the opinion of the Egyptians will be
The esteem wherein I hold my people
That when you depart, you will not go
As if altogether empty-handed;
For women will exact of all neighbors and guests
Their gold and silver ornaments
And their gold-and-silver garments, to be used
To deck out your sons and daughters. You
Will send them off garbed in Egyptian spoil. (Ex 3:14–22)

Moses remonstrated, "Suppose they will not believe me, nor
listen to my plea? For they may say, 'No! The Lord did not appear
to you' " (Ex 4:1).

What is that which you hold in your hand?

"A rod."

Throw it down upon the ground. (Ex 4:2–3)

When he threw it on the ground it was changed into a serpent,
and Moses shied away from it.

Now put out your hand and take hold of its tail. (Ex 4:4)

So he put out his hand and laid hold of it, and in his hand the
serpent changed back into a rod.

That will take place so they may believe
There did in truth appear to you
The God of Abraham, Isaac, and Jacob.
Now thrust your hand into your bosom. (Ex 4:6)

When he thrust his hand into his cloak and drew it forth, it came out snowy white, scaled with leprosy.

Now put your hand back into your bosom. (Ex 4:7)

Moses did so. When he drew it out again he found, to his surprise, that it was completely healed, in no way different from the rest of his flesh.

If they disregard you and take no heed
Of the first of these signs, they will be convinced
By the one that follows. But should it be
They will believe neither of the two signs
And will not heed your plea, in that case
You are to take some water from the river
And pour it out upon the ground.
This water you took from the river will be water
No longer, but blood that lies on the ground. (Ex 4:8–9)

Moses then endeavored to beg off from this assignment. "If you please, Lord, I have never been eloquent, neither in the past, nor recently, nor now that you have spoken to your servant; but I am slow of speech and tongue" (Ex 4:10).

Who gives to man the mouth he has?
Who is it lets him be deaf or dumb
Or sighted or blind? Is it not I,
The Lord? Go—I will assist your speech,
And will teach you what you are to say. (Ex 4:11–12)

When Moses interjected, "Pardon me, Lord, send someone else!" (Ex 4:14), God became angry.

Have you not a brother, Aaron the Levite?
I know that he is an eloquent speaker,
And he is now on his way to meet you.
In talking with him you will see that those words
Which I have spoken are put in his mouth.

I will be in the mouth of both of you,
Showing each of you two what you are to do.
Though he will address the people for you,
Acting as spokesman, yet it is you,
Not he, who will take the part that is God's.
Grasping that rod in your hands, you will work
Signs in my name. Go back to Egypt;
All they who sought your life are dead. (Ex 4:14–17, 19)

Moses Returns to Egypt

So, bidding his father-in-law good-bye, Moses set his wife and
one of his sons astride an ass and started the trip back to Egypt,
carrying the rod of God with him. And God continued to instruct
him as he went his way.

See that you perform before the Pharaoh
All the wonders I have put in your power.
I will make him obstinate, however,
And he will not let the people go.
So you shall tell him, "Hear God's decree!
Israel is my son, my firstborn.
Let my son go that he may serve me.
If you refuse to let him go,
I warn you I will kill your son,
Him who is your own firstborn." (Ex 4:21–23)

Not long afterward, when they had halted for the night, Moses
nearly met his death at the hand of God's angel because he had
not yet circumcised his son. But Zipporah saved his life. Snatching
up a piece of flint, she at once performed the rite and laid their
son's foreskin at her husband's feet.

Meanwhile, stirred by an impulse from God, Aaron had set out
through the barrens toward his brother. They met at Mount Sinai,
and Moses revealed the words and signs God had commanded to
be said and done. Together the two (Zipporah and the boy seem
to have returned to Midian) made their way back to Egypt and the

land of Goshen. There they convoked the council of Israel's elders and Aaron told the assembly of God's revelations to Moses. Moses performed the signs in the sight of the people, and they were convinced that Moses was indeed God's spokesman. The people rejoiced to hear that God was aware of the tribulations they suffered and had come down among them. They bowed low in adoration before the Lord.

The Levite brothers Moses and Aaron, sons of Amram, then obtained an audience with the Pharaoh—who, many historians agree, was Rameses II—and gave him God's command, "Let my people go celebrate a feast to me in the desert" (Ex 5:1). But the king despised the Hebrews' God as being the god of mere slaves, and gruffly denied their petition. He charged Moses and Aaron with being troublemakers. In the Pharaoh's view, the Hebrews of Goshen were his minions, to be savagely subordinated to the service of the state. Nothing was to be allowed to interfere with their workaday life.

The angry Pharaoh laid a heavier burden upon the Jews: They were now required to furnish for themselves the straw which up to that time had been supplied for their brick-making by the Egyptians. Not only that, but there was to be no reduction in the daily quota of bricks exacted of them. The Pharaoh knew that this arrangement would require more time of the Israelites, but had they not found time in their idleness to listen to troublemakers who proposed time off for sacrificing to their god?

The edict was enforced brutally. The taskmasters flogged the Hebrew foremen when the quantity of bricks fell below the quota. The Jews lodged protests with the Pharaoh in vain. They finally turned on Moses and Aaron and bitterly reproached them on account of these misfortunes.

Moses pleaded with God for relief, and God promised him that the Pharaoh would not only be punished, but humbled. He would even feel compelled to drive the Hebrews out of his realm. However, God addressed his words mainly to the Hebrew community. He repeated his most sacred name of Yahweh, saying that it was this name he wanted the tribes to use in place of "El Shaddai," the name by which the Patriarchs had invoked him.

I who am Yahweh, the Lord,
Appeared to Abraham, Isaac, and Jacob
As El Shaddai, but my name is Yahweh.
I did not make myself known to them
Under that name, but with them I made
A Covenant to give them the land
Of Canaan, where they were living as aliens.
Now hearing the groaning of the Israelites
At their being enslaved by the Egyptians,
I have remembered my Covenant.
Say this to the sons of Israel,
"I am the Lord, who will free you of labors
Imposed on you by the Egyptians.
With my outstretched arm and my mighty acts
I will rescue you from this slavery.
I adopted you as my own people,
And you shall have me as your God.
You will know, then, that it is I, the Lord
Your God, who freed you from your labors
And brought you into the land I swore
I would give to Abraham, Isaac, and Jacob,
And I give it to you as your own possession.
Yes, I the Lord will do all this." (Ex 6:2–8)

At this time Moses was eighty years of age, his brother eighty-three. And Moses, who may have been a stutterer or stammerer, expressed his bewilderment: "How can it be that Pharaoh will listen to me, poor speaker that I am?" (Ex 6:12). But the Lord again mentioned that many signs and prodigies were still to be worked by the divine power before the Pharaoh would let the people go. He told the brothers to approach the king again.

The Sending of the Plagues

In the audience that followed, Aaron threw the rod of God down in front of king and court, and it turned into a serpent. But the sorcerers of Egypt managed to duplicate the feat; the Pharaoh was unmoved and did not relent. Then the Lord God made the waters turn to blood in the Nile, the marshes, the tributary rivers, and the canals. The people had to dig holes in the Nile's banks to find drinking water. The fish died and an unbearable stench hung over the land. But the witchcraft of the sorcerers was able to simulate this blood phenomenon, and the Pharaoh still refused to bow to the Lord's edict.

One week later Aaron, following instructions the Lord gave him through Moses, raised his rod, and a plague of frogs came out of the waters and infested the land. The Pharaoh then agreed to let the Hebrews go "tomorrow," but when the morrow arrived, he took back his promise. Successive plagues then followed—mosquitoes, gadflies, a deadly livestock epidemic, and an outbreak of boils and sores on Egyptians at large, including the magicians. The magicians were unable to mimic any of these plagues.

Gradually the implacable opposition of the Pharaoh began to change. He started making partial concessions. When the plague of gadflies came he tried to get the Hebrews to offer their sacrifice to God inside Egypt. Later he said he would allow them to go into the barrens, provided they did not go far away—nothing like a three-days' journey. Then, amid thunder and lightning, God sent down a violent and long-lasting hailstorm which devastated the land, shredding the flax, barley, and wheat, damaging the trees of the countryside, and injuring animals and their keepers in the open. Although the Pharaoh now confessed that he had been wrong, still he would not grant what the Lord had asked. The God of the Hebrews then proceeded to make fools of the Egyptians in the eyes of the world.

Now, through Moses, the Lord threatened a locust plague. Since Egypt was already on the brink of ruin, the courtiers begged the king to let the Hebrew people go to perform their act of worship. The Pharaoh proposed a compromise: He told Moses and Aaron that the Hebrew men could go offer sacrifice as long as they left their wives, children, and livestock behind them as hostages for their return. Moses found this compromise unacceptable. All must go, he said, women and children and animals included. Then came the locusts; the insects devoured the field crops that had been spared by the hail, and denuded the orchards of any remaining fruits.

Again the Pharaoh called for Moses and Aaron to appear before him. The king humbly confessed to having sinned against the God of the Hebrews, but he stubbornly refused to submit to the whole of the divine command. Even when an impenetrable three-day pall of darkness fell over the whole length of Egypt, he tried another compromise: All the Israelites—men and women, young and old—could leave Egypt to worship their God, but their flocks and herds had to stay behind. When Moses and Aaron replied that the animals were needed for sustenance and for offering holocausts in honor of the Lord, the Pharaoh was incensed. In his indignation he banished the sons of Amram from his sight, forbidding them under penalty of death ever to return to the court. At that, hot with anger, Moses announced the coming of the most fearsome plague of all—the firstborn males of all the Egyptians and their domestic animals would die.

The Passover and the Exodus

The Lord now ordered the Hebrews to prepare for their exodus. A holy week was to begin with a feast of Unleavened Bread and end with a Passover meal on the day of exodus. The bread bins of the community were emptied of leavened loaves and filled with unleavened flatbread. The day of Passover was to be a most solemn commemoration of Israel's salvation from the death-plague and the nation's deliverance from Egyptian bondage. It was to be kept annually thereafter as a day of remembrance and celebration.

The Lord laid down ritual prescriptions for the Passover. The paschal victim selected for sacrifice had to be an unblemished male yearling sheep or goat. Its blood was to be collected in a basin. Then the Hebrews were to dip a spray of hyssop into the basin and mark the doorposts and lintel of each of their dwellings with the blood. The destroying angel would see the marks and pass by the Hebrew homes. No one was to venture out of doors until morning. The Israelites should roast the sacrificial victim and eat it hastily in its entirety between sunset and dark, wearing girdles around their waists and sandals on their feet, and having staffs in their hands.

That night at the hour of midnight God sent his angel to strike down all the firstborn males in the land. The heir to the Pharaoh's throne died, as did the eldest scion of each noble house, the oldest son in all other families of high or low degree, and the firstborn of all livestock. Loud wailing rose over Egypt, but not even the bark of a dog disturbed the silence of Goshen.

In the wake of this great disaster the Egyptians cringed in fear that they all might die, and the Pharaoh's courtiers begged the king to send the odious Israelites away. A crestfallen, crushed, and sorrowing Rameses II summoned Moses and Aaron and begged them to take their Hebrew tribes—men, women, children—and go. He asked in return only that the Lord God grant him the boon of peace.

The Hebrews laid a levy on the terrified Egyptian people in return for departing from the country. They demanded and received gifts from Egypt's distraught families in the shape of ornaments and caparisons—the gold and silver spoil the Lord required in cloth and metalwork. And Egypt was glad to be despoiled, as long as its former slaves would go far away into the desert to the mountain of their fearsome God.

At last the departure of the Hebrews was at hand. What a triumph God had wrought! Through his power, lowly slaves had been freed, and a proud and haughty king had been humbled. Fear of the God of the Hebrews ruled all Egyptian hearts. The year was probably about 1290 B.C.—approximately 645 years after Abraham's entry into Canaan and 430 years after the entry of the Israelites into Egypt in the time of Joseph.

The exodus involved 600,000 Hebrew men. This figure does not include their wives and children, flocks of sheep and goats, droves of cattle and donkeys, and aliens who preferred to follow the fortunes of the Israelite tribes rather than continue to endure Egyptian slavery.

Pageantry marked the miles-long column that formed: The Hebrew people made a brave show in those triumphant trappings of gold and silver ornaments and glittering caparisons that the Lord had wanted them to wear. At the head of that great file were

Moses and Aaron, the Levite brothers, to whom Egypt now deferred as lords. The women carried moistened cakes baked from the unleavened dough left over from the holy week. The men bore arms. Moses had brought with him, as holy relics, the bones of Joseph, son of the Patriarch Israel, which were to be buried in Canaan.

The column hurried as fast as possible by marches at night as well as by day; the Hebrews did not trust the Pharaoh's promise to let them go. However, the pace of progress by so vast and disordered a horde could not be but agonizingly slow. After having gone southward to Succoth and Etham, they seem to have turned back northward to reach their third campsite, which was at Pi-hahiroth near the Sea of Reeds. From Pi-hahiroth the shortest route to Canaan proceeded due east and followed the coastal road through the heavily populated land that was later to become the country of the Philistines. But because the Israelites would probably have had to fight their way through this area and perhaps lose heart, the Lord led them in a different direction.

He led them on their way himself in the guise of a pillar of mist by day and a pillar of flame by night. Afterward, the Egyptians who were tracking them thought the Hebrews to have been wandering confusedly in their flight, whereas the Cloud, which later led them straight onward, zigzagged at first in order to throw pursuers off the trail. But from Pi-hahiroth their course was to be as direct as possible to the mountain of God in Sinai.

Fickle as ever, the Pharaoh and his courtiers had soon regretted letting the Israelites go, and set out in force to bring them back. Their army was made up of the whole of Egypt's harnessed chariots, 600 picked teams of charioteers, a large corps of horsemen, and platoons of other troops. This mighty force finally caught up with the Israelites at their encampment, near Pi-hahiroth and facing Baal-zephon, between Migdol and the Sea. This was just south of the Isthmus of Suez, a narrow strip of land full of bogs, salt marshes, and lakes, now cut through by the Suez Canal. The Hebrews were terrified, fearing that the might of Egypt would fall upon their rear and destroy them. They reproached Moses: How much better to have remained slaves in Egypt than die here in the

wild! Silencing their recrimination, Moses reassured them that the
Lord would do their fighting for them.

The Cloud, which had been going before them, now swung to
their rear and checked the Egyptians' advance by making it too
dark for a nighttime march on their part. Israel had its way lit up
by the pillar of fire. Moses then lifted up his rod and a violent, hot,
and tornado-like wind blew all night long, dividing the Sea to the
right and left. The Israelite horde passed through it, over dry
ground between the watery walls, to the safety of the east shore.
At dawn the Egyptian chariots and horsemen dashed up and
plunged into this corridor, only to find their chariot wheels clog-
ging in the mire and soon unable to move. When the Egyptians
were all floundering about within the passageway, Moses raised
his rod again in the morning light, and the walls of water
crashed together, engulfing and destroying the Pharaoh's army.
The drowned bodies of the soldiers were afterward washed
up on shore.

Now, if ever, was the time to celebrate a triumph in song, and
Moses led the people:

Your right hand, O Lord, is magnificent in power!
Who among the gods is like to you?
In your mercy you led the people you saved.
Forever and ever the Lord God shall reign. (Ex 15:6, 11, 13, 18)

Then while the women with their timbrels sang and danced a
paean to God, Aaron's sister Miriam, the prophetess, led the
chorus that made up the song's refrain:

Let us sing of the Lord in the might of his glory,
Throwing horse and rider into the sea! (Ex 15:1)

The Israelites spent the next three days trudging through the
desert opposite Etham until they encamped at Marah. They were
now to suffer far greater hardships than they had undergone in
Goshen, but by these sufferings the Hebrew tribes would begin to
be molded into a nation, hard and strong.

After breaking camp they moved on, their course paralleling the eastern shore of the Gulf of Suez through the barrens of Shur and along the border of the wilderness of Sin. Here they nearly perished of thirst. They went three days without water before finding a well whose water was bitter and undrinkable; it became sweet when God told Moses to cast some wood into it. Farther on, at Elim the Israelites came across an oasis with twelve freshwater springs bowered in a cluster of seventy palm trees. However, their herds and flocks had become badly depleted in the month and a half since their exodus from Egypt. And now the Israelites began to suffer severe hunger pangs and live daily with the threat of starvation. This led them to sorrow bitterly for the pots of meat and the loaves of bread they had enjoyed in Goshen.

The Enduring Miracle of the Manna

The Lord took pity on them in their plight and began sending them some miraculous food: meat in the evenings in the form of quail, and bread in the mornings in the form of a substance at which the Hebrews cried out *Manhu?* or "What's that?" It was manna, a food sweet and tasting like honey, white like coriander seed and having the look of hoarfrost. It could be ground into a flour and turned into palatable loaves, cakes, biscuits, and wafers; or it could simply be thrown into a pot and made into porridge.

There was always enough of this food for each family to gather a supply that would meet the day's needs; and on every sixth weekday, the preparation day for the sabbath, enough to gather a two-days' supply, since no manna fell on the sabbath. Later, Moses would have Aaron place a jar of manna before the tablets of the Law, to preserve it for posterity as a testimonial.

Throughout the forty years of the slow migrations of the Israelites in the wilderness, God continued to send them manna. The manna ceased its nightly fall only after they had entered the Promised Land.

At Rephidim, a valley in the Sinai Range, the Israelites found themselves once again in a waterless region where they, and especially their children and livestock, were tormented by thirst. The people began to complain and threatened to stone Moses. God told Moses to take some of the elders with him as witnesses and strike a rock with his rod in full view of the assembled tribes. When he struck the rock, water flowed out of it. This place received the name of Massah and Meribah, "Trial and Contention," because the people had put the Lord God to the test, muttering, "Is God in our midst or not?" (Ex 17:7).

While they were still in the Rephidim area the Amalekites came down from the north to attack them. This gave the Hebrews their first taste of battle. Moses brought Aaron and Hur with him to a hill overlooking the terrain; Joshua son of Nun was put at the head of a company of picked men sent forth to engage the enemy; and Moses held the rod of God aloft on the hill. The Israelites held their own as long as Moses' arms were held upright, but when his arms began to sag, the tide of battle turned in favor of the Amalekites. All day until sunset, therefore, Moses sat on a stone while Aaron and Hur stood on either side of him, supporting his arms whenever they grew tired. At last Joshua's men cut the Amalekites to pieces with their swords and routed them. An account of that day's victory was drawn up in writing and kept as a memorial.

Years later, when the Israelites were waiting to enter the Promised Land, Moses would inveigh against the Amalekites for this malicious attack.

> Bear in mind what Amalek did to you on the journey after you left Egypt, how he harassed you along the way, weak and weary as you were, and he cut off at the rear all those who lagged behind. Therefore, when the Lord your God gives you rest from all your enemies round about the land which he is giving you to occupy as your heritage, you shall blot out the memory of Amalek from under the heavens. Do not forget! (Dt 25:17–19)

The Mountain of God

Jethro, the Midianite priest who was the father-in-law of Moses, now came up from the south. He brought with him Moses' wife Zipporah and their two sons, Gershom and Eliezer. After greeting Jethro, Moses told him how the God of Israel had delivered the Hebrews from the Egyptians and protected them in their trek through the wild. The priest of Midian then proclaimed the God of the Israelites "a deity greater beyond any other" (Ex 18:11). Jethro offered an oblation that was shared by Moses, Aaron, and the elders as a "meal before God" (Ex 18:12).

The priest then suggested that Moses, who was kept constantly busy adjudicating quarrels, appoint leaders for each Israelite grouping of a thousand, a hundred, fifty, and ten. These leaders would take the place of Moses in administration of justice for their groups. All lesser cases were to be decided by them in the future, and only the more important ones referred to Moses. Accepting the suggestion, Moses appointed men who were wise and shrewd and had been tested as leaders. Some of them were made judges, others scribes. After this, Jethro returned to his home, east of the Gulf of Aqaba.

The Israelite tribes arrived at the lofty mountain massif of the south central Sinai Peninsula three months after the start of the exodus. They pitched camp facing the mountain, a three-peaked prominence of majestic granite summits rising to elevations in feet of 6,735, 7,519, and 8,551 respectively. Christian tradition identifies the 7,519-foot eminence, known today as Jebel Musa, with Mount Horeb, the mountain of God.

This imposing mountain mass loomed up from a seemingly endless, wild stretch of sandy, rock-strewn desert. It was there that Moses had seen the burning bush and been given a summons to go and liberate God's chosen people from their Egyptian bonds. And now, an awe-inspiring theophany was about to take place there in the form of earthquakes, lightning flashes, and thunderclaps. The octogenarian emancipator was to climb those slopes several times to commune with the Lord God, his creator.

As the Israelites arrived, the mountain was wrapped in mist and was quaking; its top, darkened by a murky, thunderous cloud, was flaming to the sky. It belched smoke, and sounds like blaring trumpets were coming forth from it. As Moses approached the end of his life many years later, he gave the Israelites several vivid descriptions of the scene. He reminded the people of all that had taken place there, asking them, "Did a people ever hear the voice of God speaking from the midst of fire, as you did, and live?" (Dt 4:33). Then he recounted the awesome incident:

> You came near and stood at the foot of the mountain, which blazed to the very sky with fire and was enveloped in a dense black cloud. Then the Lord spoke to you from the midst of the fire. You heard the sound of the words, but saw no form. There was only a voice. But when you heard the voice from the midst of the darkness, while the mountain was ablaze with fire, you came to me in the persons of all your tribal heads and elders, and you said, "The Lord our God has indeed let us see his glory and his majesty! We have heard his voice from the midst of the fire and have found out today that a man can still live after God speaks to him. But surely this great fire will consume us, and if we hear the voice of the Lord our God any more, we shall die. What mortal man has ever heard, as we have, the voice of the living God speaking from the midst of fire, and survived?" (Dt 4:11–12; 5:23–26)

The people had then begged Moses to act as their mediator with God.

> Go closer Moses, and hear all that the Lord our God will say. Then tell us what the Lord tells you. We will listen and obey. Let us not hear the voice of the Lord our God, nor see this great fire any more, lest we die. (Dt 5:27; 18:6)

Moses calmed the terrified Israelites by telling them that God was teaching them fear only to keep them from sinning.

For the next six days the summit was shrouded in cloud. On the seventh day the Lord called Moses to ascend the mountain. Moses climbed up and passed into the dense cloud. God spoke to him there in a voice loud enough for all the people down below to hear it.

> To the House of Jacob say,
> To the Israelites declare,
> "You yourselves have seen
> How I treated the Egyptians,

How I bore you on eagle wings,
And brought you here to myself.
From this you know that now
If you hearken to my voice
And keep my Covenant,
You will be my special possession,
Dearer to me than all others.
And though all the earth is mine,
You will be a kingdom of priests
And to me a holy nation." (Ex 19:3–6)

The Making of the Covenant

Moses came back down to the people to obtain their endorsement of the Covenant. They swore to do God's will and to hold fast to the Law that God would lay down for them. "Everything the Lord has said, we will do" (Ex 19:8).

But preparations had to be made for the solemn act of covenanting, and two days were set aside for achievement of the proper dispositions. The people were to refrain from sexual relations, and the priests, in particular, were to purify themselves. Those who were not priests were to put on clean clothes and await a long blast from the ram's horn at daybreak of the third day, signaling God's descent upon the mountain. In addition, the Lord had forbidden man or beast to set foot upon the mountain, under penalty of stoning or arrowshots. God then called to Moses:

Come up to me on the mountain,
While I give stone tablets to you
On which I have written the commandments. (Ex 24:12)

So Moses, accompanied by Joshua, climbed to the mountain top. Moses received God's word and put into writing the Book of the Covenant, containing the Law of God. This began with the Ten Commandments the Lord had formulated.

I am the Lord your God;
You shall have no gods besides me.

You shall not carve an image.
You shall not profane my name.
You shall keep the sabbath day holy
You shall honor your father and mother.
You are forbidden to kill,
Or commit adultery,
Or take what belongs to another,
Or bear witness that is false,
Or covet your neighbor's wife,
Or anything else which is his. (Ex 20:2–4, 7, 8, 12–17)

The Book contained additional commandments bearing on slavery, homicide, and fighting; theft and restitution; rape, sorcery, and monotheism; the duty of hospitality and the care of widows and orphans; the offering of firstfruits and the rendering of honest justice; and the observance of the sabbath, the sabbatical year, and great feastdays. After writing all this down, Moses descended from the mountain.

Early the next morning Moses built an altar at the mountain's foot and erected twelve steles, or standing stones, one for each of the twelve tribes. At the altar he set youthful tribesmen who made holocausts and sacrificed young bulls as peace offerings to the Lord. Half the blood of the sacrificed animals was collected in basins. Moses sprinkled the other half, first on the altar, then on the people, as he pronounced these words:

This is the blood of the Covenant
Which the Lord, your God, has made with you
In accordance with all the words he spoke. (Ex 24:8)

Then Moses read aloud the entire Book of the Covenant, explaining to the people the various ordinances and stipulations of the compact. The Israelites expressed whole-hearted agreement with it in all its parts. "All that the Lord has said, that we will observe and do" (Ex 24:3).

At dawn of the third day there came the long blast of the ram's horn, and Moses led his trembling people out to meet their God. They made their way to the base of the mountain, which was aflame with fire and was belching a dense cloud of smoke round its summit. Out of the cloud issued dazzling bolts of lightning and deafening peals of thunder. Then the glory of the Lord came down on Mount Horeb, the mountain of God, in the form of a devouring flame. God summoned Moses to come up, and to bring with him Aaron and his two sons Nadab and Abihu along with seventy of the elders. Moses also brought his servant Joshua. They ascended together but Moses alone was to approach God. The others, though they remained on the slope and bowed low in worship at a distance, were able to see the sapphire-like flooring, clear as the heavens themselves, on which God appeared to be standing. The biblical account states that they gazed upon God, yet they suffered no harm in consequence. Before they descended, Nadab, Abihu, and the elders ate and drank on the mountain side.

Meanwhile, in the depths of the cloud, the Lord gave Moses the two stone tablets on which the finger of God had inscribed the Ten Commandments (or Decalogue). Moses was told to remain on the mountain for forty days and nights, fasting from food and drink while he received from God a complete, thoroughly detailed design for a mobile Temple. It was the divine intent that this Temple be a place of worship wherever the Israelites would happen to be in their migrations. Therefore the Temple was to be a "portable" one, constructed so that it could be taken apart and all its furniture and pieces carried off when necessary. Whenever the Cloud in which God manifested his presence would cease to hover over the Temple and move on, the people would follow it to a new campsite.

As the Temple of the divine presence, it was to have certain ideal dispositions and dimensions: It was to be situated in an oblong court, 150 feet long and 75 feet wide, which was to be screened by fencing of double-ply linen 7 1/2 feet high. A 30-foot wide gateway was to be constructed on the eastern side. The size of the court was to be large enough to accommodate 4,000 people.

The altar of holocaust, on which burnt offerings would be sacrificed, was to stand in the center of the open courtyard, opposite the entry. Behind that altar was to be a bronze basin filled with water for washing the hands and feet of the priests.

Farther back, occupying the westernmost area of the courtyard, a roofed tabernacle would stand, 15 feet high, 45 feet long, and 15 feet wide. This would be the sanctuary which none but the priests might enter. Panels of acacia wood would cover three of its sides, while the remaining east side would be closed off by a veil of richly embroidered stuffs dyed in many hues of purple. The tabernacle was to be covered by a carpet roof made of sheets of goats' hair overlaid with red-dyed rams' skins and violet-dyed leather. The dusky interior would contain a golden altar of incense, flanked to the right by a golden table of showbreads, and to the left by a golden seven-branched lampstand.

The innermost 15 feet of the tabernacle was to be reserved to the Holy of Holies, closed off by a sumptuous veil and entered only by the high priest once a year, on the Day of Atonement. In the Holy of Holies was to be an ark with a mercy seat. The ark would be a gold-plated acacia wood chest, 2 feet 3 inches high and wide, 3 feet 9 inches long. Inside it would rest the pair of stone tablets of the Ten Commandments, together with a golden urn filled with manna. On top of the ark would be the mercy seat, bearing two cherubim facing one another with upward outstretched wings. This structure was to be made of one solid piece of beaten gold. Such was to be the place where the Lord God would meet with his people and give them his word.

The Covenant is Broken

These instructions came to an abrupt end. It was an irate God who burst upon Moses with the injunction:

Get you below at once!
The people whom you brought out of Egypt
Have become depraved and are sinning.
They have cast themselves an idol;
They are worshiping a golden calf.
They are crying, "This is the god
Who brought Israel out of Egypt!"
I will now destroy this people
And make you a great nation instead. (Ex 32:7–10)

To dampen the Lord's anger, Moses pleaded:

Will you let the Egyptians say, "The God of Israel was treacherous; he led them into the mountains only to exterminate them from the face of the earth"? And what's to be said about your vows to Abraham, Isaac, and Jacob—that their progeny would rival the stars of heaven in number and inherit the Promised Land? (Ex 32:12–13)

After these words the Lord bridled his anger. Carrying the engraved tablets with him, Moses then hurried down the slope while the mountain blazed with fire behind him. On the valley floor a dreadful sight confronted him. For there, in the midst of the Israelites, stood an idol, and round its altar circled shouting, dancing people. Seething with indignation at their apostasy, Moses flung the tablets to the ground, dashing them to pieces. He grabbed the idol—a golden calf—and hurled it into the flames. Afterward, he ground it into powder, which he cast into the mountain stream that supplied the camp with drinking water. Thus the Israelites were made to drink of the idol they had made. Moses reproved Aaron severely for having listened to the people's entreaties and allowed them to lapse into idolatry—their importuning was no excuse.

Moses stood by at a gate of the camp and in ringing tones cried out, "To me, all you who are for the Lord!" (Ex 32:26). The Levites, fellow tribesmen of Moses and Aaron, rallied to his summons en masse. Then Moses bade the Levites buckle on their swords and pass back and forth between the gates of the camp, slaying brother, friend, and neighbor. That day the Levites became consecrated in the service of the Lord. About 3,000 men perished at their hands.

Moses rebuked the survivors and announced that he would go back to the Lord to see if reparation could be made for what they had done. He went before the Lord and offered to be erased from the Book of the Covenant, if that would appease the Lord's anger against the Israelites for their apostasy. But the Lord said no—only those who had sinned were to be punished; Moses should lead the people forward as he had been told. Then Moses begged God to

come with them, headstrong though they were, and forgive them
their sins and faults. But the Lord showed displeasure with so
wayward a people:

My angel will go before you.
But I shall not go with you,
Lest I wipe vou out on the way. (Ex 32:34; 33:3)

Moses was nonplussed.

You tell me to make the people go on, but you do not let me
know who it is you will be sending with me. Now if I have
found favor with you—and you did say to me, "You are my
intimate friend"—show me your nature, so that I can know
your ways and be doing what it is you want done, winning your
favor. This nation, after all, is your own people. If you are not
going with us yourself, then do not make us go up from here.
I and my people do not comprehend how we can win your favor
unless you go with us. Your presence with us would mark us
as singled out from all other peoples on the earth. (Ex 33:12–13,
15–16)

God heard his prayer and relented.

I myself will go with you,
And I will give you repose.
I will do what you request
Because you found favor with me,
And you are my intimate friend. (Ex 33:14, 17)

Pressing his advantage, Moses begged God to show himself in
all his glory. And the Lord gave his consent.

I will let my virtue pass
Before you, and I will pronounce
My name Yahweh in your presence—
I, who have compassion
And show mercy to whom I will.

But my face you cannot see.
No man who sees me can live.
Here is a place that is near me;
Stand on this rock, and when
My glory passes by,
I will set you in a rock hollow,
And cover you with my hand
While I go by. And then
I will remove my hand
So that you may see my back;
But my face is not to be seen.
Now cut two tablets of stone
Like the ones that were previously cut,
And I will write on the tablets
The words I inscribed before.
Be ready in the morning at dawn
To present yourself to me.
Ascend the mountain of Sinai,
And go to its very summit.
There is to be no one else with you,
No one anywhere
Upon the mountainside,
No herds or flocks then grazing
On the mountain's lower reaches. (Ex 33:19–24; 34:1–3)

So Moses cut two stone tablets resembling the former ones, and
early in the morning started climbing to the summit with these in
his hands. God descended upon the mountain in the form of a
cloud, and Moses stood there with him. God then passed before
him, proclaiming:

Yahweh, Yahweh, a God
Of compassion and of mercy,
Slow to anger and rich
In patience, kindness, and truth.
For thousands he maintains his mildness,
Forgives wickedness, crimes, misdeeds,

But lets evil not pass unhindered,
Punishing the fault of the father
In his children and his grandchildren
To the third and fourth generation.
I will make a covenant with you
In the eyes of all your people
And I will work marvels not wrought
Anywhere at all on earth.
Then will your people see
How awe-inspiring the deeds
Which I, your God, will do.
Let you on your part take care
Not to enter any pact of peace
With the peoples in the Promised Land;
You shall neither worship their gods
Nor marry their daughters. (Ex 34:6–9, 12, 14, 16)

It was then that God inscribed on the fresh tablets the Ten Words of the Covenant, the commandments of the Decalogue. When Moses came down from the mountain with these Tablets of Testimony engraved by God, the skin of his face was so radiant from his contact with God that the people did not dare approach him until he motioned to Aaron and the elders that he wished to speak with them. Then when all the Israelites had drawn closer, he enjoined upon them all that he had heard from the Lord. Thereafter he wore a veil over his face, which he removed only when conferring with the Lord.

The Tent of Meeting

To the assembled community Moses revealed what the Lord had said regarding the construction of his Temple, the tent of meeting which the Israelites would bring with them wherever they might be encamped. Moses must have described its general design and referred to the patterns and models of its parts as these were exhibited to him on the mountain's height. Moses also told them that the Lord had invited them to make contributions to the grand project out of their personal resources. They were invited to contribute such things as their gems and jewels; their keepsakes and treasures of gold and silver and bronze; their purple, violet, and scarlet stuffs and fine linens; their accumulations of goats' hair, red rams' hides, and fine leather; their stores of oil and spices; and their hoards of acacia wood and onyx stones.

The people were whole-hearted in their response. Morning after morning they heaped up in front of Moses piles of ornaments, finery, and valued possessions—rings, earrings, bracelets, necklaces, and polished-bronze mirrors, as well as fine-twisted linen, colored yarns, spun goats' hair, durable rams' skins, and fine leathers, not to mention stores of oil in skins and spices in cases. In fact, they proved to be so lavish in their giving that, before long, the craftsmen announced they already had more than enough materials to fill their needs.

The Lord God desired that the color of the mobile Temple's hangings, covers, and ritual vesture be in various hues of purple. Purple hues run the gamut from blue to red, trending away from the blue end of the light spectrum through such various intermediates as violet, lilac, and hyacinth, then advancing toward the red end of the spectrum through mauve, magenta, and crimson. The predominant colors used in the Lord's place of worship were the purplish hues closer to the red end of the spectrum, with crimson being favored above the others.

The pervading tinge of purple was to stand for the color of the sublime heavens, and the mobile Temple was meant to present a glorious burst of purplish-red tints in all different shades of brilliance and saturation. Such were the colors of the high, two-ply linen fencing screen round the Temple area and the veil of its gateway. Such were also the colors of the tabernacle's ceiling cover of rams' skins, of the veil at the entrance of the tabernacle, and the hangings on its walls. One could see these colors in the four-columned veil closing off the Holy of Holies, and in the various parts of the priests' and the high priest's linen vestments.

The precious metals of gold, silver, and bronze afforded a marked contrast to the purple colorings; each metal held its place in the order of its excellence. Gems and jewels contributed brilliant accents. And the dyed, fine-woven linen was frequently embellished and enriched with applications of embroidery. Always the wood employed was acacia.

The Lord himself had chosen the mastercraftsmen for the job: Bezalel for the working of gold, silver, and bronze, and for stone-cutting; and Oholiab for the damask-woven linen and its embroidery, and the making of engravings. Both these masters were to teach others their crafts.

As it turned out, it took six months for the work to get done. Huge was the amount of metal used: more than twenty-nine talents of gold, one hundred of silver, seventy of bronze. The gold and bronze all came from free-will offerings; the silver from the proceeds of a poll tax on the adult males.

The ark was gold plated inside and out, as also were the exterior surfaces of the altar of incense and the showbread table. Superimposed on the ark, the throne of mercy with its two facing angelic figures was one solid piece of beaten gold, as was true also of the lampstand base and stem, and the various ritual cups, jars, and libation bowls. Silver was used to cast a multitude of sockets, hooks, plates, and rods. Bronze platings and a bronze network covered the acacia wood of the altar of holocausts. The ablution basin was solid bronze, beaten from the mirrors of the women who would serve at the entrance to the tent of meeting. Bronze was also used to cast a vast quantity of pegs.

Throughout the six-month work period men and women labored dexterously and lovingly in carpentry, smithing, metal working, weaving, and needlework. The carpenters planed acacia wood into panels, columns, and shafts, or sawed it into posts and crossbars. The smiths at their forges plated the wooden furniture with gold, silver, or bronze. They beat or rolled gold to make the mercy seat and its angelic figures; the lampstand and ritual utensils; and the moldings, sheets, and bands. The smiths also made silver trumpets for war and for festivals. Foundrymen formed molds for networks, struts, clasps, rings, hooks, and sockets. Spinners spun goats' hair to make sheets, drawstrings, and loops. Weavers produced fine-twined and damasked linen. Dyers dipped and dried a wealth of cloth in violet and crimson-purple hues, and piles of rams' pelts in red. Needleworkers fashioned fine embroideries and created sumptuous vestments.

The Consecration of the Portable Temple

When finally all the pieces and parts were ready to be assembled, Moses blessed the workers and their work. By the Lord's ordinance the first anniversary of the exodus was set for the erection and dedication of the Temple's ensemble of court and tabernacle and for the placement of the articles of furniture. As overseer, Moses had participated in the fabrication of all the parts of the sanctuary.

Inside, the tabernacle was heavily curtained with fine linen hangings and embroideries, its dimness partially dispelled by the flames of the burning lampstand. The light from the lampstand sparkled from the exposed surfaces of gold objects and gold-sheeted furniture. The atmosphere was heavily redolent of sweet-smelling, perfumed incense.

A holy chrism was prepared from the choicest spices—liquefied myrrh, fragrant cinnamon, scented cane, cassia, and olive oil. Moses used this chrism to consecrate and anoint the tent of meeting and its contents. Within the Holy of Holies he anointed the ark, mercy seat, and cherubim. Outside the veil he anointed the altar of incense, showbread table, and seven-branched lampstand. Then, in front of the tent of meeting and out in the open court, Moses anointed the holocaust altar with its appurtenances, including the standing basin for ritual ablutions.

Finally, Moses anointed the sons of Aaron. They had purified themselves with water, the people had imposed hands on them, and Aaron had made the prescribed sacrifice to God on their behalf. But it was the anointing that made them priests. As they stood before Moses in bare feet, arrayed in sacerdotal vestments of turban, full-length tunic, and banded cincture, Moses sprinkled over them the red blood of a bullock and two rams of sacrifice. He then smeared some of the blood on the horns of the holocaust altar, and with a finger splashed more of it on the altar's sides. This

priestly ordination ceremony is graphically portrayed in the eighth
chapter of Leviticus.

In his role as high priest Aaron wore on his head the striking
insignia of his office: a miter-turban bearing a gold plate engraved
with the words "Consecrated to Yahweh." Over his tunic hung a
lengthy purple robe hemmed with hanging gold bells and with
embroideries of pomegranates. Over the robe and round his waist
he wore the woven band of the meshed linen-and-gold apron
called the "ephod." This was suspended like a scapular from
shoulder straps. The straps were embossed with twelve onyx
stones incised with the names of the twelve tribes. On his chest,
above the woven band of the ephod, Aaron wore the pectoral. This
garment was adorned with four rows of three gems inscribed with
the names of the twelve tribes and mounted in settings of gold
mesh bedecked with gold rosettes, rings, and chains of twisted
gold. It was attached to the ephod by purple ribbons.

Thus vested, Aaron must have cut a truly magnificent figure in
the sheen of his purple linen and the gleam of his jewels and gold.
What Moses wore, other than his face veil, we are not told.

To complete the ritual investiture Moses told the sons of Aaron
to cook and eat the meat from the sacrifice and to eat the bread
that was used in the sacrifice as well. For seven days and nights
they were forbidden to pass out of the entrance of the tent of
meeting; an equal amount of time was needed to complete the
consecration of the altar of holocaust.

When all this was finished, the leaders of each of the twelve
tribes presented offerings on twelve successive days for the ministry of the Levites at the altar of holocaust. Each leader brought the
following: six covered wagons with a dozen oxen to draw them;
three dozen silver bowls filled with fine flour mixed with oil for
the oblations; a dozen gold bowls filled with incense; a dozen
bullocks, rams, and male yearling lambs for holocausts; a dozen
goats for the sin sacrifices; a dozen bulls and sixty rams, kids, and
male yearling lambs for the peace offerings.

Outside the four-columned veil of the Holy of Holies, the
flames of the seven-branched lampstand were to be kept burning
all night long every night. Incense was to be burned at the incense
altar every morning and evening. Fresh loaves were to be placed

on the showbread table each week. Every day, two male yearling lambs were to be offered in sacrifice on the holocaust altar in front of the tent of meeting.*

That same year, the Israelites observed the Passover on the fourteenth day of the first month to commemorate their emancipation from bondage in Egypt. The Cloud, the visible manifestation of the presence of God among his people, appeared on the day of Dedication and covered the tent of meeting. The glory of God so filled the tabernacle that even Moses was not able to enter it, and from then on the Cloud hovered over the tabernacle—a pillar of mist by day, a pillar of fire by night.

The Departure from Mount Horeb

Moses went to consult the Lord, presumably daily, at the tent of meeting. When he did so, all the people would stand and watch at the doors of their tents. When the Cloud would drop down and station itself at the entrance to the tent of meeting, everyone would rise and bow low. "The Lord used to speak to Moses face to face, as one man speaks to another" (Ex 3:11). The voice of the Lord regularly came from the mercy seat between the winged figures of the cherubim in the Holy of Holies. On one of these occasions, God gave the Israelites orders to prepare for departure from Mount Horeb.

Moses had been told on the mountain that they were soon to invade the land of Canaan. The tribes were to proceed from Sinai toward the Promised Land "where milk and honey flow."

See, I am sending my angel before you
To guard you on the way, and bring you
To the place I have prepared. So heed him!
I will exterminate the Hittites,
The Amorites, the Perizzites,

---

*Centuries later, in a letter to Hiram King of Tyre, Solomon told of his plan "to build a house for the honor of Yahweh, my God, and to consecrate it to him, for the burning of fragrant incense in his presence, for the perpetual display of the showbread, for holocausts morning and evening, and for the sabbaths, new moons, and festivals of Yahweh, our God; such is Israel's perpetual obligation" (2 Chr 2:3).

The Canaanites, and the Jebusites,
Provided you do not worship their gods,
But worship the Lord, your God, alone.
I will bless you with bread and water there.
I will remove all sickness from your midst.
No woman will be barren or miscarry,
And I will give you a full span of life.
I will throw the nations into a panic,
Causing your foes to turn and run.
Grown in numbers, you will come to possess
All the land between the Sea of Reeds
And the Philistines' sea on to the desert,
Indeed, all the way up to the river. (Ex 23:20–21, 23–31)

The desert referred to was the Arabian; the river was the Euphrates. The territory described here actually became Solomon's empire some three and a half centuries later.

By the Lord's order a census of the people was taken according to clans and families on the first day of the second month after the Dedication. All the Hebrew men who were fit to bear arms and were twenty years of age or older were enrolled, except the Levites. When registered and assigned to battle stations, these composed a force of 603,550. Altogether there were 22,000 Levites, as reckoned in the census, but no Levites were listed and counted as part of the fighting force. They were instead designated for the Temple's ministry. There were, however, 8,530 Levites between the ages of thirty and fifty who were deemed fit to bear arms in extraordinary circumstances. Those Levites past the age of fifty were retired from active service.

When the Israelites would break camp, it was the duty of the Levites, under the eyes of the sons of the high priest, to dismantle the tent of meeting and carry the various pieces to where camp was pitched again. There they would reassemble it.

The chief assignees to this task of dismantling, transporting, reassembling, and relocating the mobile Temple were the 2,750 Kohathites. These men carried the holiest objects: the ark, showbread table, seven-branched lampstand, incense altar, ablution basin, and holocaust altar. Because of the great weight of these holy objects, the men carried them on their shoulders by means of poles. They also conveyed, on litters, the accesories of those sacred objects: the chrism, incense, oblations, dishes, cups, libation bowls, trays, snuffers, and the other ritual utensils and liturgical items, including probably the vestments.

Second in rank among the bearers were the 2,650 Gershonites, to whom was given the transfer of the tabernacle's overlay and ceiling, its hangings and the hangings of the courtyard. These included the cases of dyed leathers and rams' skins, the damasked and embroidered crimson linens, the double-ply cloth screening, and the entrance veils with their drawstrings and loops.

Third and last among the Levite porters were the 3,200 Merarites, to whom was entrusted conveyance of the framework, panels, columns, posts, sockets, hooks, plates, network, pegs, cords, and the rest of the equipment.

The Lord instructed Moses to establish certain prearranged signals among the Israelites for their sojourn in the wilderness. The sounding of the silver trumpets was to summon to the tent of meeting the tribal leaders, who were also the chiefs of Israel's battalions. A blast from two trumpets summoned the entire community and was the signal for striking camp. A blast from a single trumpet, when accompanied by the battle cry, gave the order for camp to be hurriedly broken. Successive buglings initiated the march of the tribes in a prearranged order, from the east and south of the court to the west and the north of it.

It had been settled that the tribes were always to be camped in the following order: to the east, the tribes of Judah, Issachar, and Zebulon; to the south, Reuben, Simeon, and Gad; to the west Ephraim, Manasseh, and Benjamin; to the north, Dan, Asher, and Naphtali. The Levites were to surround the court on its four sides, hence be the centermost of all the tribes. The entire camp took the form of a square.

On the twentieth day of the second month the Cloud lifted from the tent of meeting. Then Aaron and his sons said a prayer of blessing which the Lord himself had composed:

May the Lord God bless and keep you!
May his face now shine upon you!

May he be gracious to you,
And looking upon you kindly,
Thereafter grant you peace! (Nm 6:24–26)

The Israelites broke camp and set out on their march. Moses
tried to persuade his brother-in-law Hobab, the son of Reuel, to
act as the column's scout since he was familiar with that part of
the Sinai Peninsula. It is unclear from the biblical account whether
or not Moses was successful, but Hobab seems not to have accepted, as he is given no further mention as a scout.

Of the four wings in which the camp was customarily set up,
the east formed the vanguard of the march, succeeded in turn by
the south wing, the Levites carrying the tabernacle, the west wing,
and the north wing. In this first trek, however, the ark was borne
at the head of the file in order to search out the next camping place.
As they were always to do in their wandering, the Israelites moved
only when the Cloud moved, and stopped whenever the Cloud
stopped. A bright mist by day, a shining fire by night, the Cloud
halted this time at Taberah after a trek of three days. There the
people provoked the Lord: The Lord became angry at their complaining and a fire broke out that destroyed a third of the Israelite
encampment.

But apparently this did not chasten them, for at Kibroth-hattaavah, the place where they next halted and where their march
had begun to parallel the western shore of the Gulf of Aqaba, they
began complaining again. Non-Hebrews who had joined them at
the start of the exodus were bewailing the lack of the food they
had enjoyed in Egypt—plenty of meat and fish along with cucum-
bers, melons, leeks, onions, and garlic. The Israelites were stirred
up by them and grumbled about the monotony of a diet consisting
solely of manna.

Moses was put out by the sound of the wailing that was coming
from all the tents. He reproached the Lord, saying:

Where can I get meat to give to all this people, for they are
crying to me, "Give us meat for our food." I cannot carry all the
people by myself, for they are too heavy for me. If this is the
way you will deal with me, then please do me the favor of

killing me at once, so that I need no longer face this distress. The
people around me include six hundred thousand soldiers, yet
you say, "I will give them meat to eat for a whole month." Can
enough sheep and cattle be slaughtered for them? If all the fish
of the sea were caught for them, would they have enough? (Nm
11:13–15, 21–22)

The Lord answered him:

Is that beyond Yahweh's reach?
You shall see whether or not
What I have promised you
Will or will not take place. (Nm 11:23)

What happened was this: God caused a wind to blow in from
the sea, carrying with it a huge flock of migrant quail. The quail
sank down exhausted on the ground, till their bodies lay three feet
deep on either side of the camp for the distance of a whole day's
march. The people gorged themselves on the fallen birds, and in
his anger the Lord smote many of them with a deadly plague.
Because of the superabundance of quail, still more of the people
sickened of the smell of the birds and were unable to bear it.

Again Moses pleaded with the Lord, saying that his responsibil-
ity for the people was more than he could bear alone. So the Lord
had him assemble seventy of the elders in front of the tent of
meeting; coming down in the Cloud, he imparted some of the
spirit of Moses to the seventy, who thereupon began to prophesy.
Moses was very pleased: "Would that the Lord might bestow his
spirit on all" (Nm 11:29).

At Hazeroth, the next stopping place, Moses had to contend
with trouble in his family. Miriam and Aaron envied Moses the
favor God had shown him. They found an excuse to grumble
against him in the fact that he had married a "Cushite woman,"
as they derogatorily called Zipporah the Midianite.

The Lord was displeased at their turning on Moses, "by far the
meekest man on the face of the earth" (Nm 12:3). He descended
in the Cloud and commanded the two dissenters to stand before
him, as he said:

Should anyone among you be
A prophet, I reveal myself
To him in a vision or in a dream.
Not so is it with my servant Moses,
The most trusted of all throughout my house.
It is face to face that I speak to him,
All openly and never in riddles.
He lives in the presence and the sight of the Lord.
How dare you, then, engage in slander
Against my humble servant Moses? (Nm 12:6–8)

Then the Cloud went up from the tent. Turning to Miriam,
Aaron saw that she had become a leper, white as snow. With tears
in his eyes, he begged Moses not to let their sister remain in that
condition as though she were some sort of monster with half-dead
flesh aborted from their mother's womb. Moses cried to God,
"Please, not this. O heal her!" (Nm 12:13). The Lord replied:

Had her father spat in her face,
Would she not hide in shame
For seven days? Let her now
Be excommunicated
For seven days from the camp;
Only then may she come back. (Nm 12:14–15)

The Israelites remained at Hazeroth until Miriam was restored to
health.

A Reconnaissance of Canaan from the South

It was spring when the Israelites journeyed through the wilderness of Mount Paran along the foothills of the Sinai Range's eastern flank, overlooking at first the Gulf of Aqaba, and later the
Arabah Depression. Both the Gulf and the Depression constituted
a southern extension of the earth's greatest rift. Instead of going
down to the lowland, however, the Israelites turned left, crossed
to the western side of the Sinai Range, and veered north toward
the Promised Land. Within a month of their departure from

Mount Horeb, they encamped at Kadesh-barnea, with the north-
ernmost part of the Sinai Range still in sight to their right. Here
the wastes of Paran and Zin come together with no clear line of
demarcation between them; thus Kadesh is referred to at first in
the Book of Numbers as being in the wilderness of Paran, later as
in that of Zin.

Moses mentions Kadesh in the Book of Deuteronomy (1:19–
23), where he says:

> We set out from Horeb in the direction of the hill country of
> the Amorites. We had reached Kadesh-barnea when I said to
> you [the tribes], "You have come to the hill country of the
> Amorites, which the Lord our God is giving us. Go up and
> occupy it, as the Lord, the God of your fathers, commands you.
> Do not fear or lose heart." Then all of you came up to me and
> said, "Let us send men ahead to reconnoiter the land for us and
> report to us the road we must follow and the cities we must
> take." I agreed with your proposal; I chose twelve men from
> your number, one from each tribe.

The Book of Numbers vividly recounts a series of important
events that occurred while the Israelites were camped at Kadesh.
It was from there that Moses sent the twelve tribal chiefs, including Joshua and Caleb, to explore the country of the Negeb and the
highlands of southern Canaan, and to bring back samples of the
produce they found. After forty days these scouts returned with
a branch of early grapes of huge size, some pomegranates, and
some figs from Hebron's Eschol Valley. Though they had a commission to investigate the whole of Canaan, Hebron was the far-
thest north they travelled. Woven into the garbled report they
made on their return were tall tales to the effect that the sons of
Anak were as large as giants and that the Promised Land bristled
with great, fortified towns. But they did find the Negeb in possession of the Amalekites and learned that the farther highlands were
held by the Hittites, the Amorites, and the Jebusites, while the
seacoast and the Jordan Valley lay in the hands of the Canaanites.

Caleb, a prince of the tribe of Judah, was in favor of immediate,
aggressive action. But the other tribal leaders lacked Caleb's obe-

dient and bold spirit. They cringed at the prospect of fighting a
people who were alleged to be giants "who made us look like mere
grasshoppers" (Nm 13:33). In Deuteronomy 1:28 the timorous
leaders complain:

> Our kinsmen have made us faint-hearted by reporting that the
> people are stronger and taller than we, and their cities are large
> and fortified to the sky; besides, they saw the Anakim there.

The camp was demoralized and afraid; men passed the night wailing of doom, anticipating their own death and the capture of their
wives and children. A sentiment began to take shape in the
camp that new leaders should be appointed to bring the people
back to Egypt.

At this, Moses and Aaron threw themselves prone on the
ground, and Caleb and Joshua tore their garments and harangued
the rebels:

> The country which we went through and explored is a fine, rich
> land. If the Lord is pleased with us, he will bring us in and give
> us that land, a land flowing with milk and honey. But do not
> rebel against the Lord: You need not be afraid of the people of
> that land. (Nm 14:7–9)

Even so, the community buzzed with talk of stoning Moses.

Then, suddenly, the glory of the Lord shone forth at the tent
of meeting, and God intervened. The Lord threatened to destroy
the Israelite nation and make of Moses a new and greater Chosen
People. But Moses protested, pointing out:

> It has been heard that you O Lord are in the midst of this
> people; you, Lord, who plainly reveal yourself. Your cloud
> stands over them; you go before them by day in a column of
> cloud and by night in a column of fire. Now then, let the power
> of my Lord be displayed in its greatness. Pardon this people
> their wickedness as befits your great kindness, even as you have
> forgiven them from Egypt until now. (Dt 14:14, 17, 19)

Moses obtained the Israelites' forgiveness, but with this stipulation:

Not even one of them,
Save Caleb and Joshua
And the very youngest children
Shall ever see the land
I promised to their fathers.
Tomorrow you shall turn back
To the barrens of the desert
In the direction of the Red Sea.
Tell them, "In the desert
Shall all of you meet death,
For now you will be nomads.
In return for those forty days
Of faithless reconnaissance
You shall now undergo forty years
Of life and death in the wild." (Nm 14:23–25, 29–35;
Dt 1:35–40)

The Lord then struck dead the spineless tribal chieftains who had reconnoitered and yet disparaged the Promised Land.

The Israelites were dismayed at the bleak prospect of spending the rest of their lives in the wilderness. Some of them now gave belated thought to undertaking the conquest they had disdained. In Deuteronomy 1:41–46 Moses says of them:

Each of you girded on his weapons, making light of going up into the hill country. But the Lord said to me:
    You are to tell them this,
    "Do not go up and fight,
    Lest you be beaten down
    Before your enemies,
    For I will not be in your midst."
I gave you this warning but you would not listen. In defiance of the Lord's command you arrogantly marched off into the hill country. Then the Amorites living there came out against you

and, like bees, chased you. That is why you had to stay as long as you did at Kadesh.

Full of presumption, the Israelites had marched out of the camp and away from the ark, only to have the Amalekites and Canaanites rush down upon them and rout them, harrying them all the way from the highlands back down to Hormah, ten miles east of Beersheba in the Negeb.

The Rebellion of Korah

Korah the Levite was restive under the leadership of Moses and Aaron. He rebelled against Moses, and created a dissident faction of 250 Levites and two Reubenites, Dathan and Abiram. These men, persons prominent at the feasts, were united by jealousy and ambition. They said to Moses and Aaron, "Enough from you! The whole community, all of us are holy; the Lord is in our midst, too" (Nm 16:3).

When Moses heard this he first threw himself on the ground, and then rose and proposed a test. Was it not enough for the Levites to have been singled out for dedication to the service in the tabernacle and the performance of the sacred rites? Did they all have to aspire to the priesthood, too? Moses told Korah's Levites to fill their censers with fire and incense. He asked Aaron to do the same. The Lord himself would show who it was who bore the mark of divine favor and consecration.

Moses called for the two Reubenites, wishing to talk with them too, but they refused to come. They accused Moses of having brought the community out to die in the wilderness, luring them by the promise of a land flowing with milk and honey. Now "you lord it over us," they said (Nm 16:13). Enraged at their words, Moses begged the Lord to honor their holocausts no longer.

On the following day the crowd of 250 Levites, with their censers filled with incense, confronted Moses and Aaron at the entrance to the tent of meeting. Suddenly the glory of the Lord shone forth to the whole community. The Lord told Moses and Aaron to shun the company of the Israelites, for he was going to annihilate them all. Moses and Aaron fell prostrate and prayed the

Lord not to destroy all the people for the sin of one man, Korah. At that, God ordered the people to withdraw from the vicinity of Korah's dwelling and to disassociate themselves from the rebels, not touching anything belonging to them for fear of becoming involved in their sin.

When they had all pulled back in a great circle, Dathan and Abiram came out and stood with their families in front of their tent doors. Then Moses solemnly proclaimed:

> This is how you shall know that it was the Lord who sent me to do all I have done, and that it was not I who planned it. If these men die an ordinary death, merely suffering the fate common to all mankind, then it was not the Lord who sent me. But if the Lord should now do something altogether new, something utterly out of the ordinary—such as the earth opening up and swallowing them with all their belongings, so that they go down alive to the nether world—then you will know they are guilty of defying God. (Nm 16:28–30)

The instant he spoke these words there was an earthquake. The ground split open beneath the men who had rebelled, and they and everything they owned were engulfed. The multitude drew back in terror so as not themselves to be swallowed up. Immediately fire came down from God and consumed the Levites who had sided with Korah. Afterward, the Lord commanded that the bronze censers be dug up, emptied of their sacrilegious coals, and beaten into sheets with which to cover the holocaust altar. This would serve as a standing warning that none but those of Aaron's line dare burn incense before the Lord.

The next morning the Israelites began to grumble against Moses and Aaron because of the deaths that had taken place. When the people started banding together in their bitterness, the Cloud came down and covered the tent of meeting, and the glory of God shone out. God told Moses that now he was going to annihilate the Israelites for certain.

Resorting to quick action, Moses at once directed Aaron to fill a censer with incense and hasten with fire from the altar to perform the rite of atonement over the people, for God's wrath had

already taken shape in the form of a plague. Aaron raced through
the camp swinging his censer between the living and the dead.
Though the plague then ended, the lives of 14,700 fresh victims
were claimed by it.

To put an end to all such dissension, the Lord told Moses to
have the leaders of the twelve tribes bring him twelve almond
branches, each marked with the name of their patriarchal family,
and to place these in front of the Testimony in the ark. Which-
ever branch sprouted first would indicate the choice that God
had made.

When Moses came to the tent of meeting the next day, Aaron's
branch had already sprouted: There were flowers in bloom and
even fully ripe almonds. Moses returned all the branches to their
owners, and the complaining and disputes were thus quieted for
good. At the Lord's direction, Aaron's branch was placed inside
the ark alongside the Tablets of the Testimony.

The people became afraid that they were all doomed to die if
lay people dare not approach the tabernacle with their offerings.
Therefore, the Lord gave certain prescriptions for the Temple
which were put into effect. The Levites, Aaron's kinsmen, were to
serve at the tabernacle as simple oblates of the Lord. Aaron and
his sons were to be priests, concerned with the altar and with what
lay beyond the veil—in a word, both sacrifice and the rites performed in the Holy of Holies pertained to them. Thus it was made
clear that Aaron and his family of priests would care for the
sanctuary, while the rest of the Levites would be responsible for
the other parts of the tabernacle. This being so, God's wrath would
never fall on the people unless a layman should presume to usurp
such functions.

The priests were entitled to the consecrated offerings—oblations of wine, wheat, and the various firstfruits—for their food.
The firstborn among human beings was to be redeemed by an
offering to the Lord in a rite that mystically marked the child's
head as if a circlet henceforth were being worn around it. The
firstborn of cows, sheep, and goats was to become a sacrificial
offering at the holocaust altar. But while all the other tribes would
have an inheritance in the Promised land, the House of Levi would
not. The tithes they received would be their inheritance.

Much had already happened at Kadesh: the ill-fated expedition to Canaan; the sentencing of the entire generation of Israelites then living to forty years of wandering in the wild; the revolt of Korah and his Levites; and the legislation bearing on worship and the sanctity of the priesthood. But even more was still to happen. For it was at Kadesh that Miriam died, she who had been temporarily stricken with leprosy at Hazeroth. And another miracle was to take place at Kadesh.

The Forty Years of Wandering in the Wild

The Kadesh region was arid. The tribes bemoaned the wretchedness of the place where they now found themselves. Nothing could be grown there; there were neither vines nor figs nor pomegranates—and worse, no water. Moses and Aaron pleaded insistently with the Lord to provide the Israelites and their cattle with water.

So the Lord told Moses to take the rod he had used at the Pharaoh's court and at the parting of the Reed Sea, and to strike a certain rock, ordering it in the presence of the people to give out water. Moses obeyed. "Listen, you rebels," he said to the crowd, "Shall we make water come forth from this rock for you?" (Nm 20:10). Then he raised his hand and smote the rock twice. At the second blow, water came gushing forth in abundance, and the community and its cattle drank their fill. The waters became known as the Waters of Meribah—or Contention—because God had been provoked.

Perhaps the Lord had also been provoked by Moses and Aaron. Should Moses have struck the rock only once? The Bible does not tell us. At any rate, the Lord spoke to Moses and Aaron in these words:

Because you had no faith
That I would reveal my virtue
To the House of Israel,
You shall not lead this people
Into the Promised Land. (Nm 20:12)

Since Israel had hesitated to invade Canaan from the south, the side that was the most direct, the Lord now forbade them to enter the Promised Land from that side. So they had to turn their attention to the possibility of finding a route northward by skirting the Dead Sea on its eastern flank. They hoped to travel by way of the king's highway through the mountainous countries of Edom and Moab.

Therefore Moses sent a message to the king of Edom, petitioning the right of way needed by the Hebrew people. The letter mentioned the hardships the Hebrews had endured in Egypt and their deliverance by an angel of God, and it stated that they had now arrived at Kadesh, a town near the border of Edom. Jephthah in the Book of Judges (11:17) states that Moses sent a similar message to the king of Moab requesting unmolested passage through that land, and received a similar reply.

The Edomites were Esau's descendants, just as the Moabites were Lot's descendants, and Moses might well have looked for an affirmative and sympathetic reply from these, his remote kinsmen. It is likely that Joshua was his spokesman. But though Moses promised that the Hebrews would not cross any fields or vineyards or disturb any wells, and that they would keep to the king's highway, turning neither to the left or right of it, the king of Edom flatly refused his request. "You shall not pass through here!" he said (Nm 20:18). He added that if the Hebrews attempted to pass through anyway he would advance against them with the sword. Further negotiation proved fruitless. The Edomite monarch marched out in force to his frontier to see to it that the Israelites did not trespass.

The Israelites seem to have spent about two years at their first camp in Kadesh. Though the events that happened there are dwelt upon at length, Moses does not mention their first sojourn at Kadesh in the meticulous listing of the camps made during the exodus (Nm 33:3–49). In Deuteronomy, however, after he states that the Israelites had remained at Kadesh for a long time (1:46) Moses says that "thirty-eight years had elapsed between our departure from Kadesh-barnea and the [Wadi Zered] crossing" (2:14). So no doubt two of the forty years which Israel had been condemned' to spend in the desertlike lands had been passed at Kadesh.

The tribes had been blocked from making headway toward the Promised Land—from the south by a divine prohibition, to the east by Edom's hostility. For this multitude of people with their hundreds of thousands of animals to attempt to cross the Dead Sea was, of course, unthinkable. Israel was therefore doomed to years of wandering in the desert wilderness south of the Dead Sea. This area was a hundred-mile long, inhospitable region stretching from the Dead Sea to the inlet of the Red Sea called the Gulf of Aqaba. It comprised the Arabah Depression, the foothills and plateaus of the Sinai Range to the west, and the mountains of the Seir Range to the east.

The Bible cites the names of the various places where the Israelites stayed during this time, but the length of their stay at these places is not recorded. The twenty-three camping sites listed by Moses for the forty years after their departure from Hazeroth to the arrival at Iye-abarim in Moabite territory were: Ritmah, Rimmon-perez, Libnah, Rissah, Kehelathah, Mount Shepher, Haradah, Makheloth, Tahath, Terah, Mithkah, Hashmonah, Moseroth, Bene-jaakan (where there were wells), Gidgad (elsewhere called Hor-haggidgad), Jotbathah (where the wadis had streams of water), Abronah, Ezion-geber (at the head of the Gulf of Aqaba), Kadesh (in the wilderness of Zin), Mount Hor (on the border of the realm of Edom), Zalmonah, Punon, and Oboth.

As Moses said to them later, "Your God was training you as a man trains his child" (Dt 8:5). In Dt 8 and Dt 29 Moses recounts how the Israelites had meandered listlessly for a lifetime, wandering through a vast and terrible wasteland infested by fiery vipers and scorpions, where they suffered intolerable pangs of hunger and thirst. There had been no wine or beer to drink, and no bread to eat; they had lived on manna, a strange food which neither they nor their fathers had known, but by which they came to understand that "not by bread alone does man live, but by every word that comes forth from the mouth of the Lord" (Dt 8:3). In that parched and arid land the Lord had caused water to flow from a rock to prove to them that he was their God even in adversity. Remarkably, in all those forty years their clothes did not fall away from their backs in tatters, nor did their sandals wear out or their feet swell.

But now, by God's orders, they had returned to the wilderness and were wandering for what must have seemed an interminable number of years. At Ezion-geber they had come to the king's highway, but they could not follow it northward because of the hostility of Edom. Thereafter they found themselves back at Kadesh for a second time.

Arad, a Canaanite kinglet in the Negeb, discovered that the Hebrews were approaching Mount Hor by way of Moseroth. Arad attacked them and took some prisoners. What were the Israelites doing in that vicinity? Were they probing southern Canaan again to find out whether or not God still forbade them to attempt the conquest of the Promised Land from that direction? There is no telling, though God did give them victory in this encounter with Arad; but only after the Israelites had vowed to lay under ban the towns they captured. This meant that the spoil that fell to them at Hormah and the surrounding settlements became the Lord's property, not their own. The victory over Arad constituted a religious conquest, marking the fact that the Israelites were finally embarked on the initiative which would eventually result in their occupation of Canaan.

After the second stay at Kadesh, the Israelites had moved back again into the depths of the wilderness, traveling to Moseroth and Mount Hor. There Aaron, who was three years older than Moses, died at the age of 123. The Israelites buried him on that mountain. He had outlived his eldest sons Nadab and Abihu, who had died because of their involvement in Korah's revolt. Another son, Eleazar, succeeded him now as high priest. The people dressed Eleazar in his father's vestments. The whole house of Israel then spent thirty days mourning Aaron's death.

On the Way to the Promised Land

A turning point in the history of the nation had been reached. For Aaron's death marked the passing of that whole generation, except for Moses, Joshua, and Caleb, which had taken part in the exodus from its beginning at Goshen. This was the fortieth and final year of wandering to which Israel had been sentenced. A second, new generation, raised on the miraculous gift of manna and hardened by adversity, had grown to maturity. They were now to undertake their warrior destiny in the quest for Israel's inheritance—the Promised Land.

The twelve tribes departed from Mount Hor and traveled northward toward the Dead Sea. For the Lord had told them:

> Long enough have you wandered through
> These highlands. Now is the time
> To turn and go to the north! (Dt 2:3)

Somewhere along the line of their march—perhaps at Zalmonah, Punon, or Oboth— the people grew impatient once again, complaining about their lack of food and water. God chastized them by allowing serpents to creep in among them. The stinging, burning bite of these vipers brought death to many. Then Moses mounted a bronze serpent on a standard, and anyone who suffered snakebite was saved if he gazed at it.

It must have been later, at Oboth, just west of the kingdom of Edom and in the initial stage of their northward march toward the Dead Sea, that the Lord gave the Israelites these directions:

> You are about to pass through the dominion
>   Of your kinsmen the descendants of Esau,
> Who inhabit the Seir and are fearful of you.
>   Take care that you do not disturb them;
> For I will not give you any part of their land,
>   No, not so much as a foot,
> For the heights of Seir were long since assigned
>   To Esau as his estate.
> You must pay in money for what you eat,
>   And pay for what water you drink.
> Blessed have you been by the Lord your God
>   Throughout your long migration:

You have been his concern these forty years,
    You have never been in want. (Dt 2:4–7)

Moving swiftly now on the wings of anticipation, at the foot
of the Dead Sea the Israelites turned due east and headed up the
gully of the Wadi Zered. There they pitched camp at Iye-abarim,
on the boundary between Edom and Moab. The Lord gave them
further instructions:

You will go and skirt the land of Moab
    Toward the Ammonite frontier.
You are not to attack the Moabites;
    I will give you none of their land,
Seeing it belongs to the sons of Lot.
    Breaking camp, you are to cross the Arnon;
For I am putting Sihon the Amorite,
    The king who is seated at Hesbon,
And all of his country into your hands.
    You are going to down him in battle;
And from that day on, fear and dread of you
    Will panic the peoples at large;
Those hearing the rumor of your approach
    Will quake in their fear and terror. (Dt 2:18–19, 24–25)

The Israelites had passed Edom on its western side, and now
they cut sharply to the east and passed Moab on its eastern frontier. They crossed the Ar River and approached the Arnon, the
southern border of the Amorite kingdom of Sihon. From Kede-
moth, somewhere east of Moab, Moses sent envoys to the Amorite
king at Heshbon. These conveyed sentiments of peace together
with an application for free passage on toward the Jordan. Sihon
not only refused Moses' request but marched out in strength to
Jahaz to give the Hebrews battle as they advanced from their last
camp at Dibon-gad. Sihon's host was routed, and his cities, one
after another, were captured and plundered. His subjects were put
to the sword and their livestock carried off. Heshbon, the Amorite
capital, became a Hebrew stronghold. From there the Hebrews
ruled the region extending from the Arnon River north to the

Jabbok River, and from the border of Ammon west to the Dead Sea and the lower Jordan.

Another Amorite kingdom remained, however. Farther to the north, across the Jabbok, was the land of Bashan, and on this the Israelite divisions now marched. Og, the king of Bashan, engaged them at Edrei on the border of Gilead, and the Israelites won a resounding victory. Og's army was cut to pieces and sixty high-walled Amorite towns, among them the capital, Argob, fell to the Hebrews. The victors also captured the open towns of the Perizzites.

In the wake of the overthrow of the two Transjordanian kingdoms, Israel held dominion from the gorge of the Arnon up as far north as snow-capped Mount Hermon, ruling all the lands lying immediately east of the Jordan. We are not informed what the yield of plunder was from the two Amorite realms, but, judged by the later yield from Midian's conquest, it must have been enormous.

Near the middle of the thirteenth century B.C. the Israelites moved from an encampment on the Abarim Range down to the Plain of Moab. Despite its name, this plain was not Moabite territory when the Israelites came to occupy it, as it had belonged to the Amorite kingdom of Sihon. It designated a sloped tableland stretching from the slopes of Mount Pisgah, known also as Mount Nebo, to the northeastern shore of the Dead Sea and the place where the Jordan River flowed into it. The Hebrews named their campsite on the Plain of Moab "Shittim," which means the "Acacias." It was there that Moses had his headquarters. Within sight, only a few miles away on the other side of the Jordan, was the palm-fringed city of Jericho.

It was understandable that the king of Moab would grow apprehensive at the presence of the seemingly invincible Hebrew nation not twenty-five miles from his frontier in the valley of Beth-peor. The Israelites had crushed his neighbors; might they not, with their hundreds of thousands of fighting men, turn on Moab as well? The king of Moab looked frantically for an ally in the south, and apparently getting no response from Edom, he came to an understanding with Midian.

The Prophecies of Balaam

Aram, "the land of two rivers," lay about 350 miles from the capital of King Balak of Moab. Nonetheless, it was to Pethor on the Euphrates that the king and his Midianite allies sent off a delegation to speak with the renowned prophet Balaam, son of Beor. Balak asked Balaam to come and lay a curse on the threatening Hebrew hosts. The Patriarchs had held Aram to be their family's native land; and Balaam, the prophet from Aram, will be found addressing God as El Shaddai, as the Hebrews' ancestors had. The delegation offered Balaam a tempting fee and assured him of their confidence that "whomever you bless is blessed and whomever you curse is accursed" (Nm 22:6). Balaam at first refused to come, however, because the Lord forbade him to curse the Hebrews. King Balak sent him another, more pretentious mission with a still more handsome bribe, but again the prophet declined to come. "Even if Balak gave me his house full of silver and gold," he said, "I could not do anything contrary to the command of the Lord my God" (Nm 22:13). Later, it seems, the Lord advised him to go, provided that he would follow the divine instructions given him. So he saddled up his ass and set forth.

Could it be that he was not wholly to be trusted? Could this have been what caused the Lord's wrath to flare up at his departure? For somewhere along the road an angel stood with drawn sword to bar Balaam's way. Balaam's ass saw the angel, but Balaam did not. The ass turned off the path and Balaam beat her to try to force her back. Then the angel stationed himself in a narrow lane between two vineyard walls. Conscious of the angel's presence, the ass brushed against a side wall and grazed Balaam's foot, for which he beat her soundly. Next, the angel posted himself in a still narrower section of the path where there was not enough room to avoid him. The ass fell down under her master with all fours folded under her. Balaam became furious and mauled her with his stick.

At that moment God gave the animal the faculty of speech. The ass complained, "You have beaten me three times. Why?" Balaam replied, "Because you have been making a fool of me. If my hand held a sword, you would now be dead." Then God removed the veil from Balaam's eyes so that he saw the angel brandishing his sword, and the angel spoke to him. "I am here to hinder your passage. Had the ass not seen me, it is you who would now be dead." "I did not know," said Balaam, "so I will go back." "No," was the reply. "Go on accompanying the party, but say only what I tell you to say" (see Nm 22:29, 32–35).

When the prophet told King Balak, "I can speak only what God puts in my mouth," (see Nm 22:38), a sacrifice was held and Balaam participated in it. The prophet was led up to a lofty crag from where he could see the cloud of dust that was rising at the back of the Hebrew camp. There on the crag he offered holocausts of seven bulls and seven rams at seven different altars. Then, leaving the king with his chieftains at the altars, he himself withdrew to consult the Lord. When he came back, he uttered a poem in which he wondered:

How curse when the Lord does not?
May my end be like unto theirs! (Nm 23:8, 10)

The king became angry and led the prophet to a place high up on Mount Pisgah which overlooked the entire camp on the tableland below. Again holocausts were offered on seven altars, and again the king and his party were made to wait while the prophet went aside to consult the Lord. Balaam returned, and this time he said:

A blessing I am to pronounce;
To withhold a blessing is beyond me.
No omen exists against Jacob,
And none against Israel. (Nm 23:20, 23)

Though sadly disappointed, the king still remained hopeful. "Let me bring you to another place where it may please God to let you curse them" (Nm 23:27). He took the prophet to the peak of Peor. There for the third time a bull and a ram were sacrificed on seven different altars. This time Balaam, knowing that it pleased the Lord to bless Israel, did not go apart to perform a divination. Turning his face toward the wilderness and raising his eyes to heaven, he had a vision of the twelve tribes dwelling in peace in their tents. Seized by the spirit of God, he broke into this lyrical song:

An oracle from the closed eyes,
From one who hears God's word
And sees what the Lord discloses—
One who swoons and his eyes are opened.
How lovely are your dwellings, O Jacob!
And your tents, O Israel!
Amid gardens on the banks of a river,
Your homes are established by God.
Like cedars growing near brooks
Their progeny is well-watered.
Their king will conquer Agag
And wipe that kingdom from earth.
God brought them out of Egypt.
They are strong as the wild ox;
They will devour their foes,
Whose bones they will have broken,
Their bodies riddled with arrows.
They are like a sleeping lion,
Like a lioness which none dare awake.
Blessed are all who bless you,
Accursed are all who curse you! (Nm 24:3–9)

King Balak beat his palms together in frustration. "I summoned you here to curse my foes, and you have blessed them three times instead. I promised to reward you handsomely. But now be off! Your Lord has withheld the reward from you" (Nm 24:11). Balaam refused to depart until he had prophesied once more:

Jacob is like a rising star;
Israel wields the scepter.
Moab and Edom lie smashed.
Israel exults in strength,
Jacob becomes a master;
Amalek is defeated forever,

The Kenites become captives of Asshur.
Ships sailing the sea from Kittim
Will put down the kingdom of Asshur
And lay waste the Habiru.
All these, too, in the end will perish. (Nm 24:17–24)

Moses later recounted this incident to the assembly of Israel:

Moab hired Balaam son of Beor from Pethor in Aram Naharaim
to curse you. But the Lord would not listen to Balaam, and
turned his curse into a blessing for you, because the Lord your
God bore love for you. (Dt 23:5–6)

The king and the prophet parted from one another, and Balaam,
as we shall see, proceeded down to Midian.

The Monotheism of the Hebrews

Though Balaam is here seen consorting with pagans, his God
was the God of the Hebrew Patriarchs. Among the sons of Lot in
Moab, and the sons of Abraham by Keturah in Midian no memory
of El Shaddai remained. The inhabitants of Moab and Midian now
worshiped nationalistic Baals, that of the Moabites being the god
Chemosh.

But the Hebrews had always revered El Shaddai, though they
now used for him the name of Yahweh which he had revealed to
them forty years earlier at Sinai. For the Israelites, all other gods
were false gods; to worship them was paganism. Yahweh was the
one true God who had spoken to their forefathers, chosen them
from among all the nations on earth, and made a covenant with
them at Mount Horeb. They were dedicated to his worship alone.
Their God was a jealous God; he tolerated no pagan practices
whatsoever. The Hebrews used no images in their worship and
were bound to obey the enactments that Yahweh laid down for
them. "The Lord your God is the God of gods, the Lord of lords,
the great God, mighty and awesome" (Dt 10:17).

In the Temple of the Israelites a tabernacle sheltered the focal
point of worship. The Holy of Holies contained the ark which, in

turn, housed the Tablets of the Covenant and supported the mercy seat. The tabernacle extended out over the incense altar and the lampstand opposite it, and it faced a courtyard in which stood the holocaust altar. Priestly attendants made the sacrificial offerings. To worship God at any other place or in any other way constituted an abomination. The stringent tenets of monotheism were hard for a primitive people to learn; yet only one God existed, and to that one God the Hebrew people were bound by their Covenant.

The exodus had severed the Israelites from direct contact with the false gods of Egypt. When they had tried to resort to the paganism familiar to them from their life in Egypt by setting up a golden calf at Mount Horeb, Moses destroyed the idol. During the forty years which followed they milled about in the barrens of the Arabah, out of reach of infidel influence. Thus they were exposed neither to temptations to marry outside their own people, nor to the allurements of false worship.

Now, however, conditions had radically changed. For here at Shittim the Israelites were dwelling in the midst of pagan nations. In particular, they were having close contact with Moab and its Midianite allies. The Lord had warned them:

You shall have no gods except me;
Nor shall you make yourselves
Any image that is carved.
I, Yahweh your God,
Am full of jealousy.
You shall not give in marriage
A daughter or son of yours
To a profane family. (Dt 5:7, 9; 7:3)

But Hebrew men were now involving themselves with the sacred prostitutes at the high place of the Baal of Peor. These Midianite women invited them to banquets of pagan worship. The Lord burned with anger at their unfaithfulness. A plague broke out in the camp and 24,000 people died. God told Moses to stake the leaders of the tribes out in the broiling heat of the sun as a punishment for their failure to watch over the people and keep them from sinning. The judges (perhaps the same tribal chiefs) then saw to it that all who had allowed themselves to be perverted by the women of Midian were executed.

The matter drew to a climax when a Hebrew named Zimri of the tribe of Simeon flaunted his infidelity by leading a Midianite woman named Cozbi, who was the daughter of a clan chieftain, to a trysting tent. He did this right under the eye of Moses and in full sight of the assembly gathered in front of the tabernacle to bewail the spread of the plague.

Unable to abide so brazen an affront to the Lord, Phinehas son of Eleazar left the Temple courtyard and followed Zimri to the trysting place, where he found the Hebrew man and pagan woman locked in a close embrace. He ran the two of them through with his lance. His act of zeal was rewarded with a proclamation assuring him that the priesthood would always be the mark of his descendants and that the rite of atonement would be reserved to them.

In retaliation for their intrigues, the Lord commanded that the Midianites be assaulted and struck down. Thus they would be punished for the curse on Israel that they had sought through Balaam and for the perversion of Israelite men that had been achieved through the Midianite women. So Moses called up a force of 12,000 men, 1000 from each of the twelve tribes. Phinehas the priest was with them, carrying the sacred vessels and the battlefield bugles. This detachment then went forth to engage the enemy.

The victory fell to the Israelites. All Midianite males were put to the sword, including five chieftains who had been Sihon's vassals or had lived with the Amorites. The prophet Balaam, who was found among their number, was also killed. The women and children were taken captive, the livestock was seized as booty, and the towns and camps were pillaged, sacked, and burned to the ground.

Moses went out to meet the troops as they made their way back to camp with the spoil. He upbraided the officers for not executing all the male children and the women (except for women who were virgins). All the soldiers who had killed anyone or had touched a corpse were made to stay outside Israel's camp with the prisoners for seven days. During that time they purified themselves and their booty. Objects made of gold, silver, bronze, iron, tin, or lead

were passed through fire and then through water; then the clothing of the soldiers was washed.

The sack of the Midianite kingdom yielded an enormous profit
for Israel: close to 675,000 head of sheep, 72,000 oxen, and 61,000
donkeys. They took 32,000 virgins captive. The spoil was divided
equally among combatants and civilians. The combatants tithed
every five hundredth animal or woman to the temple priests. The
civilians turned over every fiftieth animal or woman to the other
Levites. The officers—commanders of a thousand, commanders of
a hundred—voluntarily gave the plundered jewelry over which
the rite of atonement had been performed to the Temple. This
included armlets, bracelets, signet rings, earrings, and brooches,
the gold content of which came to 16,750 shekels.

Israel on the Eve of the Conquest

At Shittim the Israelites were standing at the door of the Promised Land in exceedingly great numbers. During their forty years
of wandering in the wilderness they had suffered disastrous losses
of life: at Taberah, where a third of the people's tent dwellings
burned to the ground; at Kibroth-hattavah, where a plague had
afflicted the community; at Kadesh, from where the unsuccessful
sally against southern Canaan was made, and where several hundred rebels and their families were buried alive in Korah's rebellion; in the later skirmishes with which the religious war of
conquest of Canaan had begun; on the border of Edom, where
many were fatally snakebitten; and in the widespread battling to
subjugate the two Amorite kingdoms.

The Bible reports the military strength of the tribes both at
Mount Horeb and on the Plain of Moab. We learn of the latter
from a census taken there by Moses and the high priest Eleazar.

At Mount Horeb it had been reckoned that there were 22,273
Levites one month old or older. There were 8,580 Levites between
the ages of thirty and fifty who were able to bear arms. On the
Plain of Moab the total number of Levites was 23,000. Thus there
should have been about 9,000 of them then able to bear arms.

At the census taken on the Sinai Peninsula the number of
fighting men from the eleven other tribes (no Levites being

counted) was 603,550. On the Plain of Moab the census showed 601,730 fighting men (exclusive of Levites) on the eve of the invasion of Canaan. Though all the soldiers registered in the earlier census had died (except for Moses, Joshua, and Caleb) Israel's present warrior strength was approximately as great as it had been forty years before. This is remarkable, considering that some of the soldiers had been executed for apostasy at Peor, and others must have died among the 24,000 people struck down by the plague at Peor. Battle losses sustained in the overthrow of the two Amorite kingdoms must have been extraordinarily light.

The primary purpose of the census taken on the Plain of Moab was to divide up the Promised Land for settlement by the tribes. The territory that had been promised to Israel by the Lord stretched northward from the southern end of the Dead Sea and from Kadesh-barnea, where the wildernesses of Paran and Zin met, to Lebanon and snow-hooded Mount Hermon, and from there northeast to the Euphrates River. The land extended west from the Mediterranean to the plains and highlands of Transjordania. Not all of the promised area was to be occupied by the Hebrews at once; total fulfillment of the promise would await the kingdom built by David and the empire ruled by Solomon.

The Bible usually refers to the Promised Land by the name of "Canaan." Technically, however, Canaan was only the principal part of the Promised Land, that is, the part embracing the central Palestinian highlands and their slopes, on the one side down to the Mediterranean, and on the other, down to the Jordan and the Dead Sea. Much of Canaan proper became the home of the Philistines (hence our name "Palestine").

The distribution of tribal property rights in the Promised Land began with the partitioning and allocation of Transjordania. The former Amorite possessions east of the Jordan (between the River Arnon and the River Jabbok) were sought after by the tribes of Reuben and Gad, who specialized in sheep and cattle raising. They believed these plains would make ideal grazing grounds. Before Moses gave them permission to settle there, however, they had to pledge to cross the Jordan and fight alongside the other tribes in the conquest of the rest of the Promised Land. They were first given time to construct forts, sheepfolds, and corrals for their wives, children, and livestock.

A similar allocation of land, this time the plains and highlands between the Jabbok and Yarmuk Rivers (Gilead), was made to the half-tribe of Manasseh. Manasseh was also given rights to the tableland of Bashan.

The remaining tribes were to find their rights across the Jordan as the territory was conquered and occupied. The larger portions of land were to go to the more numerously populated tribes. This dividing would be done by lot, the lots being cast later under the eyes of Joshua, successor of Moses, and the high priest Eleazar.

The Levites, however, were to have no particular section of the country assigned to them for their inheritance. They were instead to be given a place of their own within each one of the tribal sections. This place would consist of a town and surrounding pastures. In addition, they were to be granted six "cities of refuge," three in Transjordania and three in Canaan. These cities would be towns where men who had committed involuntary manslaughter could flee for asylum. Altogether, a total of forty-eight towns, more from among the larger tribes and less from among the smaller, were to belong to the Levites.

Women never inherited property except in the case of a family that had no male issue. Moses laid down the rule that they should then marry within one of the clans of their paternal tribe. In this way the land rights of one tribe were never to be alienated to another.

The Book of the Law

It was at Shittim that Moses wrote the Book of the Law, which reaffirmed the Sinai Covenant and laid down the rules that were thereafter to govern Hebrew life and worship. The Book of the Law was a compilation of the divine ordinances given to Moses during the forty days and forty nights he spent on top of Mount Horeb. The first item treated in the Book was that of the fidelity and reverence owed to God. Since the twelve tribes were about to cross the Jordan and begin their occupation of Canaan, it had to be deeply impressed upon them that there was to be no desertion of their God, no following after pagan gods "that cannot see or hear, eat or smell" (Dt 4:28). Anyone heard urging them to serve other gods was to be stoned outside the camp. No Hebrew was ever to make a carved image, whether of man, beast, reptile, bird, or fish, or fashion a representation of the sun, moon, or stars. Living in a world that was idolatrous to the core, the people were prone to depart from the worship of the one true God and begin to follow after idols. The Lord alone was to be the object of their veneration; and he was a jealous God, a consuming fire whose anger could blaze out in a moment.

Furthermore, the Lord was to be worshiped only in his Temple, the place that he chose as a home for his name. Offerings would be burned and peace sacrifices made on the holocaust altar in the tabernacle's courtyard. There the Israelites were to bring their tithes of firstfruits, their firstborn sons, and firstborn animals. Their sons would be redeemed, but the animals would be sacrificed. Both would be presented to the Lord in this way to acknowledge the utter dependence of the Hebrews upon their God.

A long-range set of administrative provisions for the Hebrew community made up the bulk of the Book of the Law. The people were enjoined to keep the sabbath holy by refraining from all work. There was to be an appointment of judges and scribes. Three times a year the men were to appear before the Lord: at the feasts of Unleavened Bread, Weeks, and Tabernacles. Every year during the month of Abib, all of the people were to keep the feast of Unleavened Bread and the Passover sunset meal to commemorate their deliverance from bondage in Egypt. Each year, at the time of the wheat harvest, the people were to celebrate the feast of Weeks. Every year, at the time of the threshing-floor and winepress harvest, they were to keep the feast of Tabernacles. Every seventh year at the feast of Tabernacles the Law was to be read in the hearing of the entire community.

If distance were ever to prevent some of the Israelites from bringing to the Temple once a year a tithe of the produce of their land with which to celebrate as the Lord commanded, they were to be allowed to turn their tithes into money, then travel to the Temple, purchase equivalent oblations for sacrifice, and celebrate. The ritual of the tithing ceremony called for the Israelites to bow down while the priest presented their offerings to the Lord. They were to recite a certain formula of thanksgiving:

> My father was a wandering Aramaean who went down to Egypt in small numbers to take refuge there; he came out a strong and mighty nation. It was the Lord who brought us to this land where milk and honey flow. Here now do I contribute firstfruits from the soil which the Lord has given me. (Dt 26:5–10)

The oblation was always to be proportionate to the bounty with which God had blessed them. Nothing blemished or unclean was ever to be used. Every third year the tithes could be laid at the door of their own homes as gifts for the poor, the term "poor" meaning the orphans, widows, Levites, and strangers. All the poor were welcome to join their fellow Hebrews in keeping the feasts.

Stern rules were incorporated in the Book of the Law which covered the details of life in the community. The Book contained many ethical and moral precepts which embodied a high degree of charity and justice. It prescribed that help be extended to a brother in distress. It was solicitous of the poor, commanded that justice be not denied them, and insured that leavings from field and vineyard harvesting would be given them. The Law dictated honesty in men's dealings, forbade bribes to be offered or taken, and prohibited the use of short or long measures of weight. It outlawed feuding and blood vengeance. It allowed sentence of capital punishment by stoning or hanging to be passed on a man only for his sins, and limited corporal punishment by flogging to forty strokes of the lash. It condemned both female and male prostitution, declared transvestism unlawful, and strongly opposed fornication, adultery, rape, and kidnaping. The Book of the Law showed marked concern for the treatment of escaped slaves and for the prevention of cruelty to animals. For instance, an ox and donkey were not to be harnessed together as a ploughing team, nor an ox to be muzzled while treading wheat, nor a mother bird to be killed when taking eggs from her nest. The Law ordered the return of lost goods and strayed animals. It also required that parapets be installed to guard against accidental falls if roofs were ever used for living purposes.

Many of the rules in the Book of the Law dealt, of course, with what was distinctive of Hebrew life and worship. A legal defilement resulted from the eating of certain foods, for example, scavenger birds or beasts, some predators, and carcasses of wild animals found dead. Impurity also resulted from touching a human corpse. This condition was undone by certain ritual ablutions or by the simple passing of time.

Vows were to be fulfilled as soon as possible, interest not exacted from members of the community, and a birthright not transferred from a firstborn son to the son of a favored wife. A man was obligated to marry his brother's widow, and a husband not to remarry his divorced wife if her second husband had divorced her or left her a widow. Murder cases were to be judged by a Levite priest, as also were instances of leprosy. Evidence of a young woman's virginity was to be kept by her father in order to protect her good name and reputation. Participation in public worship was denied to the Ammonites forever, and denied to the Edomites till the third generation. Illegitimate or defective offspring were ineligible to take part in the worship of the community.

Good order required that the Levite in the town not be neglected, cloth not be partly wool and partly linen, tassels be worn on the four corners of one's cloak, the blood of the sacrificial victims not be drunk but poured out on the ground, trespassers be allowed to pluck grapes or ears of corn when passing through a neighbor's field provided they carried nothing away, and men be free in indignation or grief to tear their clothes but not to gash their bodies or shave their heads.

At this moment the Israelites were still on the far side of the Jordan across from Jericho. Moses called an assembly of the twelve tribes and read to the multitude the Book of the Law, teaching them the enactments and customs that they and their descendants were to keep from that day on.

This command which I enjoin on you today is not too mysterious and remote for you. It is not up in the sky, that you should say, "Who will go up in the sky to get it for us and tell us of it, that we may carry it out?" Nor is it across the sea, that you should say, "Who will cross the sea to get it for us and tell us of it, that we may carry it out?" No, it is something very near to you, already in your mouths and in your hearts; you have only to carry it out. (Dt 30:11–14)

This Law, Moses said, was not beyond their strength. They should have it on their tongues and in their hearts. Moses knew that at the dedication of a firstborn son the Israelites had the custom of wearing handbands and headdresses of circlets; well, let them now wear excerpts from the Law instead, and inscribe words from the Law on their gates and doorposts. "What great nation is there," he asked, "that has its gods as near as our God is to us?" (Dt 4:7).

The Lord was a merciful God who would never forget the promise he had made to his people. As long as they obeyed his commandments scrupulously, he would never destroy them; rather, he would bless their offspring, the produce of their soil, and the issue of their herds and flocks. He would love them more than all other peoples, for he had chosen them for his very own out of all the people of the earth. His heart was set on them; it was for love of them that he had given the oath sworn to their fathers. The Lord was a gracious God, ever true to his Covenant for the good of those who sought to love and obey him.

Moses' Parting Exhortation

Did ever a people, Moses declaimed, hear the voice of the living God and remain alive, as they had heard it speaking to them from the heart of the fire? This had taken place so that the Israelites could see that the Lord indeed is God, that he, and no other, is truly God in heaven above as well as on earth below. If they listened to his voice and followed to the end the way marked out for them, they would prosper and live long in the rich land they were going to possess. "You shall love the Lord with all your heart, with all your soul, and with all your strength. Let those words be written in your heart and repeat them to your children" (Dt 6:5).

Should they fall from the grace and love of God, the Lord's curse would come down on them for infidelity to the Covenant. A ruthless alien nation of unintelligible speech would invade the Promised Land and besiege their towns. The Israelites would be reduced to eating one another's flesh and they would suffer from horrendous plagues. The handful of survivors that remained would be uprooted and scattered among the nations. They would suffer from worn feet, tired eyes, halting breath, and quaking heart. Life would become an insupportable burden to them.

However, were even the full weight of the curses to come upon them, Moses wanted the Israelites to remember that God still loved his people. When all this will have come to pass (for Moses' exhortation was prophetic), and wherever God may have driven them among the nations, the way would be open for them to return to the Lord. If only they meditated on the blessing and the curse set before them and obeyed the Lord's voice with all their heart and soul in everything enjoined on them in the Law, God would then redeem the captives and take pity on his people. He would gather them together from among the nations and bring them back to the land of their fathers. They would make it their own again and enjoy a prosperity even greater than that of their fathers.

Moses then began to speak of the immediate future. God was now going to bring them into the prosperous land lying across the Jordan, a land of running waters, wheat, barley, vines, figs, pomegranates, olives, oil, and honey. There they would have all the bread they yearned for; there they would find iron ore and copper deposits. It was a much different land than the one they had known in Egypt—not a flat land watered by treadmill, sluice, and irrigation methods, but a land of hills and valleys watered by rainfall that came in good season to grow grass for their grazing animals, corn, wine, and oil. They had every reason to bless God for this land he was giving them. They would have fine homes to live in, and plenty of silver and gold. They were about to cross the Jordan and conquer a land flowing with milk and honey. The Lord had laid it under the ban and was putting it into their hands. The Israelites should remember that the victories they were going to win would be the work of the Lord alone. They would have cities they did not build, well-furnished houses they did not put up, wells they did not dig, and vineyards and olive groves they did not plant. But they must never forget their God, the God who had delivered them from bondage in Egypt, shepherded them for years in the wilderness, drew water from rocks for them to drink, fed them with manna, and now had caused their numbers to rival the stars of heaven.

Moses exhorted the Israelites to fear the Lord, swear by his name, cling fast to his commandments, and have nothing to do with the gods of the pagans around them. And in the future, when a son would ask, "What is the meaning of the decrees, laws, and customs laid down by the Lord?" his father would tell him, "Once we were Pharoah's slaves in Egypt, but the Lord with a mighty hand brought us out of Egypt, ordering us to observe these laws" (Dt 6:20–24). For Yahweh is the God of gods and Lord of lords, the great, triumphant, and terrible God, never partial, never to be bribed. The Hebrews had proof of his love when he turned the attempted curses of Balaam into blessings.

So now a blessing and a curse were set before them—a blessing if they obeyed this Law, a curse if they followed other gods and left the way marked out for them. The burning question was, Would they cleave to the Covenant with their God and stand clear of the ways of the pagans? Would they have no carved idol in their midst, set up no standing stones and sacred poles, use no spells, charms, and enchantments, indulge in no divinations and sorcery, have no recourse to consultations with the spirits of the dead, nor participate in the ritual of passing through fire? If doubts beset them, they would have prophets, who were to be listened to if their prophecies came to pass.

Moses turned to the warriors of Israel, hundreds of thousands strong, and gave them their marching orders for the invasion. There were commanders of hundreds and of thousands of fighting men, and there were priests to make the proclamation: "The Lord goes with you! Have no fear!" (Dt 20:4). Once across the river, they were to smash the idolatrous standing stones wherever they found them set up, cut down the sacred poles, burn the raised idols, and tear apart the altars set up on high places or under spreading trees. For a soldier to appropriate to himself the gold and silver plating of the idols would be to violate the ban, with bitter and poisonous results. In all events, discipline had to be observed; no one was to follow the dictates of his own heart.

Rules for the siege and capture of towns were drawn up. Since the Promised Land lay under ban, the rule was death to all the living. Outside this territory, if their enemies agreed to capitulate peacefully they would be allowed to live and serve the Israelites as forced laborers. If resistance was offered, the penalty was death by the sword for the men, and captivity for the women. The livestock was to be confiscated, the town sacked, and its contents heaped up for a flaming bonfire in the public square. Should a siege prove long and bitter, the Hebrew attackers were free to fell any sort of trees for scaffolding and firewood except fruit trees.

With the passing of time, it would become the Hebrew custom to grant exemptions from military service. In particular, any man who was newly married was to be released from all military obligation for an entire year. Before a battle was joined it was to become the practice for the scribes to announce that freedom from fighting would also be granted any man who had built a house but not yet lived in it, or planted a vineyard that had not yet borne fruit; this same privilege would be granted for the man who confessed himself a craven coward.

Moderation of this sort, however, would never be extended to Israelites found flaunting the trappings of a pagan way of life. Instead, they would be put under the ban: They would be killed, and their town burned and left a ruin for all time.

For now, however, there could be no thought of exemptions from military duty. Every able-bodied man was to be pressed into service. Moses explained that the conquest might take a very long time. This was desirable, as a matter of fact, so that the depopulated countrysides would not be taken over by prowling wild beasts. (And the conquest actually remained incomplete until the time of David.) The army could expect its advance to be slower when it engaged an enemy who used horses and chariots. This is what eventually happened when the Israelites met up with the Philistines.

After Moses had committed the Law to writing and made it into a book, he turned the volume over to the Levite carriers of the ark of the Lord's Covenant. He said to the Israelite assembly:

Take this scroll of the Law and put it beside the ark of the Covenant of the Lord your God, that there it may be a witness against you. For I already know how rebellious and stiff-necked you will be. Why, even now, while I am alive among you, you have been rebels against the Lord! How much more, then, after I am dead! Therefore, assemble all your tribal elders and your officials before me, that I may speak these words for them to hear, and so may call heaven and earth to witness against them. For I know that after my death you are sure to become corrupt and turn aside from the way along which I directed you, so that evil will befall you in some future age because you have provoked the Lord. (Dt 31:26–29)

Moses then ordered that the tribes pause when they reached the Shechem Valley, between Mount Gerazim and Mount Ebal, so that the Book of the Law could be read to them, proclaiming blessings that would be their lot if they were faithful to the Covenant, and curses that would fall on them if they rebelled.

Moses Relinquishes Command

On the first day of the eleventh month of the fortieth year of the exodus, Moses told an assembly of the tribes, "I am now one hundred and twenty years old, and am no longer able to move about freely" (Dt 31:2). Moses knew that he was not to cross the Jordan, but would die on its eastern side. He appointed judges to administer justice for each thousand of the people, and then prayed the Lord to designate a new leader in his place. The Lord chose Joshua son of Nun, who as a young man had ascended Mount Horeb at Moses' side and had been his aide-de-camp during the entire time in the wilderness. Joshua was "a man in whom the spirit dwells" (Dt 34:9).

The Lord told Moses to summon Joshua and inform him of the decision. Then the Lord said that the two of them should come and stand together at the tent of meeting so that Joshua might receive his orders. When they did so, God came down in the form of a pillar of fire. Later, in front of the whole assembly, Moses and the high priest Eleazar imposed hands on Joshua. Moses then relinquished his authority. And from that time on, all Israel obeyed the new leader, a prince of the tribe of Ephraim, a brave soldier and a clever strategist.

The Lord told Moses to write a farewell song of warning to the Israelites:

Soon you will rest with your fathers,
And this people give wanton worship
To other gods that are false,
The gods of the land of their conquest.
They will break the Covenant,
The one that I made with them.
My anger will flare up against them.
I will leave them to themselves
While I hide my face from them
And adversity devours them.
For they will encounter a host
Of evils and afflictions.
Now at that time they will say,
"If disasters like this could befall us,
Surely our true God is not with us!"
But upon that day my face
Will stay veiled and hidden from them,
On account of the crimes they committed
In adhering to those other gods.
Write them, therefore, this song
And teach it to Israel's sons
Until they have learned it by heart
And can sing it loud and clear.
It will be a canticle
Of warning to Israel's sons
That I was the one who brought them
Up to the land I had sworn,
A land flowing with milk and honey.

They will eat, be filled, and grow fat;
They will turn to other gods
And give them willing service,
Humiliating me
And voiding my Covenant.
But by then many sufferings and sorrows
Will have overtaken them.
Ever to be a reminder
Upon the lips of their offspring,
This song will serve to warn them
That I know temptations they toy with
And this very day yield to,
Even before I have brought them
Into the Promised Land. (Dt 31:16–21)

So Moses wrote the song known by his name—the Song of
Moses. With the elders and the scribes gathered round him, he
taught its verses to the full assembly of the Israelite people.

Now heaven and earth give heed
To the words that come from my lips!
May my teachings fall like soft rain,
My counsels be beads of dew
Or showers greening the grass.
I call upon God's name
And invoke the great grandeur of God.
For he is our rock of perfection,
Whose judgments all prove to be right.
A faithful God is he,
Without any semblance of wrong,
Even-handed and never unfair.
But his sons are soiled with sin,
And are a perverse generation.
Is such the return you make him,
The father of your being,
By whom you were made and preserved,
O you foolish and senseless people?
Think back to the days of old;

Reflect on days gone by.
If you ask your sire, he will tell you,
And old folks will echo his words:
The Most High, in allotting mankind
Its inheritance by nations,
Was mindful of Israel's numbers
And their portion as the people of the Lord.
God fastened a tether to Jacob,
Found wandering aimlessly
In a vast, horrid, and empty desert,
And led him to and fro,
Guarding and training him,
Like the apple of his eye.
As an eagle that circles its nest
And hovers over its fledglings,
Screaming to them to fly,
And spreading its wings to buoy them,
Strong pinions to hold them up,
God bore him thus on his shoulders.
There was none but the Lord to guide Jacob;
No foreign gods were at hand.
God brought him to tablelands
To eat of the yield of their fields.
There he suckled honey from a rock,
Some oil from the flintiest crag;
There he lived on butter from cows
And on milk that he got from his sheep,
On fat from his ewes and rams
Of a stock that is bred in Bashan,
On he-goats, with wheaten meal;
And he drank the pure blood of the grape.
Jacob grew fat and got stubborn,
Like some gross and bloated tumor.
He deserted God, his creator
And abandoned God, his savior.
He provoked the Lord with his idols
And his damnable practices,
And spurred God's wrath to fury.

For he sacrificed to demons,
Renownless divinities,
Who are godly nonentities
And late-come novelties,
Never revered by his fathers.
(Ah, you have left God who begot you,
And forgotten the rock of creation!)
Looking down on his people in anger
That his sons and daughters provoke him,
The Lord said, "I will hide my face
And see what the end will be
Of a dissembling generation.
My children have lost their faith,
Vexed me with hollow godheads
And irked me with nothingnesses.
I will treat them as a non-people,
As a hollow-headed nation.
They have lit a fire to my anger
That will burn to the depths of earth,
Consuming its vegetation
And the underpinning of its mountains.
I will shoot them so full of woes
My quiver of arrows will empty:
Their death will be by famine,
Or birds with the foulest of beaks,
Or the fangs of wild beasts,
Or the venom of slithering reptiles.
They will be slain by the sword in the streets.
Sheer terror will reign in their homes,
Obsessing both youth and maid,
Haunting babe at the breast and the ancient.
I would have ground them to dust
And blotted out their name from remembrance,
Were it not for the insolence
Of their haughty but deluded foes,
Who would boast that they, not the Lord,
Had brought all this about.
What a shortsighted nation, this!

Unwise and devoid of prudence!
Not knowing or understanding
What is their destiny!
For one cannot rout a thousand,
Nor two put ten thousand to flight.
Is it not that God their rock has sold them,
And their Lord has given them over?
Let their foes then judge for themselves:
Those vineyards were the vineyards of Sodom,
Those groves the groves of Gomorrah,
Where the grapes were poisonous grapes
And the fruit set teeth on edge.
That wine was the venom of serpents,
The death-dealing bane of cobras.
Yet Israel to me is still precious,
A gem stored in my treasury.
But vengeance is mine and reprisal;
So the moment they make a misstep,
Then doomsday is at hand,
And near is the time of their ruin."
But even as he sits in judgment,
The Lord takes pity on his servants,
For he knows that their hands are weak:
Hampered, they lose their grip,
Exhausted, they waste away,
No longer of avail.
"Where now," God will say, "are those gods
In whom they put their faith,
On whose victims' fat they feasted
And whose wines of libation they swilled?
Let those come, if they can now, to aid you
And provide the protection you need!
But know that I Am Who Am,
And there is no God but me.
It is I who dispense life, dispense death;
It is I who afflict and heal;
There is none who lives free of my power.
Yes, I raise my hand to heaven

And swear that I live for ever.
My sword-blade flashing like lightning,
My hand seizing the cudgel of justice,
I shall repay all my foes
As well as all who hate me.
My arrows will drink of blood,
My sword be glutted with flesh,
With the gore of those slain or captured,
With the heads of hostile chiefs."
Let all the tribes of his people
Now praise him who exacts revenge
For the blood of his faithful servants,
And repays their foes in full,
As he blesses the land of his people. (Dt 32:1–43)

The Death of the Emancipator

His life's work done, that day Moses was told by the Lord:

Climb up to the top of that mountain
Which is part of the Abarim Range,
And behold the land of Canaan.
When you have seen it you
Will be gathered to your people
As Aaron your brother was.
For both of you rebelled
In the wilderness of Zin,
When the tribes complained against me;
When I had given you orders
To proclaim my holiness
Before them by means of the water. (Dt 32:49–51; Nm
27:12–14)

Moses blessed the tribes and then turned his steps away from
the Plain of Moab and toward the 2,500-foot high Pisgah peak of
Mount Nebo. He climbed the slope of the mountain and made his
way up to the summit.

It was a breathtaking view of the Promised Land that could be seen from this mountaintop. From there the aged eyes of Moses looked northward across the breadth of Gilead to the land that Dan would come to occupy. He looked westward across Jericho to where stretched the Judea and Samaria of the future, and the Mediterranean Sea. He looked southward across the Dead Sea to the expanses of the Negeb and the wildernesses. How the eyes of Moses must have feasted on this panorama!

And there on the Pisgah height, his illustrious life of almost a century and a quarter in the Lord God's service came to a close. The Israelites buried his body in a secluded valley, where it would never be found by heathens. The people mourned his death for thirty days before they crossed the Jordan and launched the invasion.

Never was there such a prophet in Israel as Moses, the man of God, the man familiar with God, who knew and spoke with the Lord face to face. Never were there such signs and wonders as those God worked through him before the Pharaoh and his servants. The nation of Israel had been shaped by Moses; he was its organizing spirit, its religious leader, its earliest legislator. With him Israel made its appearance on the stage of history approximately 3,225 years ago.

CHAPTER SIX

JOSHUA

Joshua

At Jericho, Ai, and Shechem

The Lord himself gave Joshua orders and encouraged him.

Be brave, be full of valor!
So that you may give to this people
Possession of their Promised Land.
For that, I shall be at your side. (Jos 1:5–6)

As supreme commander of the Hebrew nation Joshua son of Nun now laid his plans for the conquest of Canaan. The invasion was to start with the overthrow of the ancient walled city of Jericho, a stronghold which guarded the passes to the western highlands. This place had been a center of human habitation since the Neolithic Age; we know from archaeological evidence that Jericho was contemporary with the earliest village settlements in Mesopotamia, where the story of human culture and the recorded history of mankind begin. To gather intelligence of the area and the town, Joshua dispatched a pair of young men as scouts who would reconnoiter the countryside and enter the city as his secret agents.

Joshua's spies entered the city and stayed at the house of Rahab, a harlot. When the king of Jericho learned of their presence there, Rahab saved them from capture by his soldiers. The two scouts pledged to her in return that she and her kinsfolk would not be harmed when the assault on the city came. She told them how things stood in Jericho, namely, that the town's defenders were paralyzed with fear because of the nearness of the Israelites, and tales told of all the help the Israelites had been given by their God. Before leaving, the spies cautioned Rahab to mark her window with a scarlet cord to alert the Hebrews not to disturb her dwelling when they entered the city. Then Rahab let them down by a rope through her window (the house was part of the city wall), and they escaped.

The spies reported all that had happened to Joshua, who now set his host in motion, evacuating Shittim and pitching camp on the bank of the Jordan ford. Three days later, officers circulated throughout the camp with marching orders. The column was to follow after the Levites who would carry the ark through the ford.

It was early spring, the time of year when the melting of the snows on Mount Hermon overflowed the river's banks and spread out over the lowlands. On this occasion, however, something very extraordinary happened: The Jordan stopped flowing past the point where the Israelites wanted to cross. The ark and its bearers stood still at midstream while the tribes passed hurriedly and dry-shod to the other side. Joshua ordered twelve men to each take a boulder from the river bed and plant them at Gilgal as a memorial to God's action in allowing them to cross the river on dry land. Joshua told the people, none of whom except Caleb had witnessed the parting of the Sea of Reeds, that it was "just as the Lord your God had done at the Sea of Reeds" (Jos 4:23).

There, at Gilgal, the Hebrew nation made its first camp in Canaan on the tenth day of the first month of the year. Gilgal lay on the plain two miles east of Jericho and two miles west of the river, which was now flowing again as usual after the Israelites' passing. Word that they had accomplished the crossing of the Jordan spread like wildfire among the Canaanite tribes, who lived in dread of the forthcoming attacks.

To make ready for the conquest, Joshua had the nation renew its Covenant with the Lord. This was done by a renewal of the rite of circumcision among the Hebrew men. None of them had been circumcised while wandering in the desert, for they could not endure it and be constantly on the move at the same time.

At evening on the fourteenth day of the same month the Israelites observed the Passover, and on the next day they ate the produce of the land, taking it in the form of unleavened bread and roasted grain. And from that day on, the manna which had sustained them in the wilderness fell no more; henceforth they were to live upon the plants and animals the Promised Land provided.

By now the men's wounds had healed, and Joshua moved his host against Jericho. The city had barricaded its gates and shut itself up within its wall. The Lord placed Jericho and the whole of Canaan, except for Rahab and her kin, under ban. This meant death for its inhabitants and consecration of its valuables to the Lord.

God instructed Joshua how he wanted the Israelites to attack. Once each day for six days the Hebrew column, with the ark and seven priests at its head, was to make a circuit of the town in utter silence, returning at night to the camp. On the seventh day the circuit was to be made seven times, at the end of which all bedlam was to break loose. The priests would blow their ram's-horn trumpets and the soldiers sound the war cry. These directions were carried out to the letter, and at the final explosive outburst the walls of Jericho collapsed. The Hebrews rushed in and massacred all, save Rahab and her kin, and then put the town to the torch. The Lord had given Jericho into their hands, and Joshua laid a curse against its ever being rebuilt.

But one of the Israelites had secretly violated the ban. Joshua discovered this when he led the Hebrew forces up into the highlands to attack the town of Ai eleven miles above Jericho and was defeated.

Etymologically, Ai means "the ruin," and archaeological evidence shows that the place was indeed a ruin in Joshua's day, probably serving as an outpost of the town of Bethel only a short distance away. Thus, while the Book of Joshua speaks only of Ai, we should understand this name to refer to Bethel in reality.

In any case, the place was reconnoitered by Hebrew scouts who reported that it could easily be taken by a small detachment. Accordingly, 3,000 soldiers were sent to attack it. They were defeated. In great distress Joshua implored the Lord to come to the aid of his people. The Lord told him that the reason for the defeat was that one of them had committed a serious sacrilege. This man had to be found and punished. Joshua called for an assembly of the tribes, and the sinner, a man named Achan of the tribe of Judah, was brought to confess his guilt. He had kept for himself a fine robe of Shinar, 200 shekels of silver, and a gold ingot, and had hidden these inside his tent. Achan was taken to a nearby valley where he was stoned and all his belongings destroyed. A great cairn was raised over him and his remains to serve as a warning to Israel for the future.

After this incident the provisions of the ban were relaxed to allow the troops to appropriate ordinary goods and cattle as their spoil, and Joshua was allowed by the Lord to resume the campaign against Ai. During the night Joshua had 5,000 fighting men take up a concealed position not far west of Ai. Meanwhile, he led the main body of his force to the far side of a ravine just north of the town. In the morning, the men of Ai came out to engage their assailants, thinking to rout the Israelites as easily as they had done before. Joshua let his army be driven back, feigning flight toward the wilderness. Then, when the town's defenders had been drawn off, the Hebrew contingent west of the place rose from ambush, entered, and captured the unguarded settlement and set it on fire. Joshua's fighters then turned back and fell upon their pursuers. Counting those who fell dead on the field and the inhabitants of the town, some 12,000 of Ai's people died. Their chieftain was captured and hung, and the town was left a ruin.

Now a conquering nation, Israel next traveled twenty-two miles northward across the highlands from Ai to the Shechem Valley. It was there that Moses had commanded them to solemnly proclaim the Blessing and the Curse. Shechem was already a place of great historic value for Israel. Abraham and Jacob had each built an altar there, and Jacob had purchased from the inhabitants of Shechem the land covered by his encampment. It was then that for the sake of a marriage alliance the townspeople had allowed themselves to be circumcised, but Jacob's sons massacred them in revenge for the rape of their sister Dinah. Before his departure from the area Jacob had buried Rachel's stolen household idols under an oak tree there. Now, centuries later, the invading Hebrew people, themselves only lately circumcised, made a momentous reaffirmation of their Covenant with the Lord.

Between the facing slopes of Mount Gerizim and Mount Ebal they built an alter of rough, undressed rocks, and flanked it with tall, plastered stones on which they had written the words of the Law. At this altar they offered holocausts and joyously partook of peace offerings. The Book of the Law was read to the assembly in its entirety, including the blessings and the curses. Then, as half the tribes gathered at the foot of Mount Gerizim and half at the foot of Mount Ebal, Levites ascended the two slopes and shouted out from the one mountain the blessings set down in the Book of the Law, and from the other mountain the curses. Thus the people were presented with a momentous choice, a choice between keeping their Covenant with the true God and defecting to the pagan gods. Blessings shouted from one mountain, curses echoing from the other—a more dramatic portrayal of Hebrew freedom to serve the Lord their God or sin against him could scarcely be imagined!

The Gibeonites and the Rest of Canaan

At the report of the muster of the Israelites at Shechem for dedication to their God, the kings of Canaan's highlands, lowlands, and maritime plains joined in an alliance against them. The Gibeonites, however, resorted to trickery instead.

Gibeon was a confederacy of Hivite towns—Gibeon, Chepirah, Beeroth, and Kiriath-jearim—communities situated in the highland west of Jericho. They played a ruse on the Israelites by appearing at Joshua's camp at Gilgal as envoys from a distant country intent upon engaging the Israelites in a peace treaty. It certainly seemed that they had made a very long journey: They had dust-covered donkey caravans, wineskins that had burst and been sewn up again, sacks that were patched in various places, threadbare garments that hung in tatters, and bread that was dried and crumbling. And they alleged that all their belongings had been new and fresh when they had left their land. Joshua and the elders were taken in by them. Not having tested the truth of their story by consulting the oracle of the Lord, the Israelite leaders broke bread and swore a treaty with them. Three days later it was learned that the Gibeonite communities dwelt in the nearby highlands. But a treaty had been made, and because a treaty was something sacred the Israelites did not abjure it.

Though the Gibeonites had become exempt from the ban and were therefore not destroyed, they were made serfs of Israel and of Israel's God. Henceforth they were to hold the menial rank of wood-cutters, water-bearers, and servants of the Hebrew rites of worship.

Despite their inferior status the Gibeonites were now allies of Israel. So when the Amorite kings of five of the highland settlements—Jerusalem, Hebron, Jarmuth, Lachish, and Eglon—made a concerted attack upon the town of Gibeon, some five miles northwest of Jerusalem, Joshua was called upon to come to its aid. The Israelite army made a forced march at night from the Gilgal camp and took the Amorites by surprise. They repelled and hurled them southwestward across the heights, panic-stricken and demoralized. A storm arose that cast great hailstones upon the Amorite fugitives, killing many of them. In order to have enough daylight to complete the rout, Joshua called upon the sun to stand still in the sky. Meanwhile, the five kings had hidden themselves in a cave. Joshua discovered this and ordered that they be taken out and hanged. Hebron and the other towns were then besieged and their inhabitants put to death.

Caleb, the faithful scout who had first reconnoitered the Promised Land, received Hebron as his inheritance. In concert with Joshua he drove the Anakim out of all their strongholds above the Mediterranean maritime plain. Joshua's conquests stretched from Kadesh-barnea through the Negeb, and over to the area of Gaza.

Under the leadership of the king of Hazor, the kings of northern Canaan formed a league against Israel. Joshua came upon them unawares while they were encamped at the waters of Merom and utterly destroyed them: Their horses were hamstrung, their chariots burned, and the king of Hazor captured and put to death. The decimated host fled demoralized toward Sidon. The Israelites were now the masters of almost the entire country. Only a few isolated pockets of resistance remained: The Jebusites could not be driven out of Jerusalem, and there were still some Anakim at Gaza, Gath, Ashdod, Askelon, and Ekron. The land of Phoenicia also remained unscathed. The Hivites lived in subjection to and in peace with Israel in their Gibeonite enclave.

The tabernacle of the ark of the Covenant was erected at Shiloh, a highland settlement ten miles south of Shechem on the highway to Bethel, and it remained there as a shrine for the Hebrews' worship and a symbol of their unity. The Promised Land was partitioned among the twelve tribes, and each tribe proceeded to settle in its allotted territory.

The Transjordanian tribes, Reuben, Gad, and the half-tribe of Manasseh stopped on their way home at the memorial stones near the Jordan ford and built an altar. This roused animosity in the other tribes, who thought that their brethren across the Jordan were forsaking their God. But the eastern tribes explained that the structure they had built was not an altar for the offering of holocausts or other sacrifices; rather, it was nothing more than a monument to commemorate the fact that the Transjordanians were still an integral part of Israel despite their geographical separation. The western tribes, who had been ready to go to war over the matter, were satisfied with this explanation and kept the peace.

The Covenant Renewed

Joshua lived to the age of 110, and was buried at his town of Timnath in the hills of Ephraim. As he was nearing the end of his days, the venerable old commander led the Israelite assembly at Shechem in reaffirming the Covenant, and exhorted the tribes to be forever faithful to God and fulfill what was written by Moses in the Book of the Law. The Lord then addressed the Israelites through Joshua:

Of old your ancestors,
Terah, Abraham, and Nahor,

Had their homes beyond the river
Where they served other gods.
But Abraham your father
I brought from beyond the river,
And led him into Canaan.
There I multiplied his descendants,
First raising up Isaac to him,
Then Jacob and Esau to Isaac.
To Esau it was that I gave
The mountain country of Seir,
Whereas Jacob and his sons went down
And entered the land of Egypt.
It was I who sent Moses and Aaron
To plague Egypt with the signs
And miracles I worked there,
To bring you out of that land
In the persons of your forefathers,
Who then fled to the Sea of Reeds
With the Egyptians in hot pursuit,
An army of chariots and horsemen.
But Israel called on the Lord,
And he spread a thick fog between you
And your Egyptian pursuers.
Then he made the sea swallow them.
The things that I did to Egypt
You saw with your own eyes.
Then for a long time you wandered
In the desert, after which
I brought you into the land
Of the Amorite peoples living
On the far side of the Jordan.
When these waged war with you
I gave them into your power,
And you occupied their country
And put them all to the sword.
Next, Balak son of Zippor,
The king of Moab, arose
To contend with Israel,

And Balaam the son of Beor
Was summoned to come and curse you.
But I would not listen to Balaam;
Therefore, he had to bless you,
And I saved you from his craft.
Then when you forded the Jordan
And came to Jericho,
The townsmen took arms against you,
As had the Amorites
With their allies the Perizzites;
As did also the Canaanites,
The Hittites, and Girgashites,
The Hivites, and Jebusites.
All these I put in your hands.
There were hornets sent out by me—
It was not your sword and bow
That ejected the Amorite kings.
You got land where you had not toiled
And towns that you had not built,
With vineyards and olive groves
You had not planted yourselves. (Jos 24:2–13)

Joshua told the people that they now had to choose whether to
worship the one true God, the strange gods their fathers had
known beyond the river, or the Amorite gods of the land where
they now were living. "As for me and my household," he said, "we
will serve the Lord our God" (Jos 24:15b). And the Israelites
all agreed, "Amen! We too will serve the Lord and obey him"
(Jos 24:24).

CHAPTER SEVEN

THE JUDGES

Judges

The Civil War

The century and a half following Joshua's death was a time of transition for the Hebrew people. They were changing over from a nomadic way of life to a sedentary one. They put away their tents and settled in the towns of a land that was now theirs by right of conquest. They still kept flocks and herds, but they also planted fields and vineyards.

This idyllic life was shattered, however, by the outbreak of civil war and by recurring threats of invasion. Adding to the troubles of the Israelites was the pervasive decay of their religion and morals.

Once Joshua was gone, this decay set in swiftly. Already during the lifetime of Phinehas, the high priest, a terrible civil war had been provoked by a crime of inhospitality (a very serious offense among the Hebrews), accompanied by debauchery. Eleven of the tribes had pitted themselves against the twelfth, and had almost totally annihilated it. This is what happened.

A Levite was traveling to Jerusalem with his concubine, and stopped along the way at the town of Gibeah to spend the night. Gibeah was just a few miles from Jerusalem, still within the southern confines of Benjamin. Late that night some scoundrels from the town tried to attack him, flagrantly violating the rule of hospitality. They compounded that evil with a heinous sexual offense: They dragged the Levite's concubine out into the open and raped her all night long. The next morning she was discovered dead on the doorstep. The Levite was beside himself with rage. He carried her corpse back to his home, hacked off its members, and sent pieces of the body to all the tribes in order to call attention to the horrible crime that had taken place at Gibeah of Benjamin.

The other tribes gathered at Mizpah on Benjamin's northern border and listened to the Levite make his accusation, "they raped her to death" (Jgs 20:5). All of them then swore in the presence of God that they would never again give their daughters in marriage to the men of Benjamin. In addition, they sent an ultimatum to the tribe of Benjamin demanding that the Gibean culprits be turned over to them for execution. But the obstinate Benjaminites refused to honor the demand—not only that, but they mustered in force at Gibeah and prepared for war against the rest of Israel. Though theirs was not a large tribe, it had battlers who were ambidextrous in their use of martial arms, and had sharpshooters who could sling stones at a hair without missing. The fighting men of Benjamin were brave, and they were confident.

The eleven tribes moved to Bethel, where they besought the Lord about battle strategy. They were told that Judah should offer battle first. But on two separate days the Benjaminites repulsed attacks on Gibeah, and the Israelite coalition sustained heavy losses. The Israelite army then fasted a day in the presence of the ark of the Lord at Bethel, and they built an altar, offering holocausts and partaking of peace offerings. Phinehas besought the Lord once again, and the Lord directed them to march against Benjamin. This time they feigned a retreat and drew the defenders out into the open country. The main attacking body then fell upon the town, took it, and burned it, putting the inhabitants to the sword. The Benjaminite force that had sallied out from Gibeah saw their town in flames behind them. They broke ranks and ran for cover to the wasteland, where their few survivors holed up at the Rock of Rimmon.

That day the tribe of Benjamin had lost 25,000 brave men; only 600 Benjaminite men were left. The tribe had been reduced to a mere remnant. The Israelite allies scoured the whole country, killing all whom they found alive. Yet the men at the Rock of Rimmon held out for four months.

Then the Israelites, sorrowing that an entire tribe should be destroyed, made peace with their adversaries. They decided to restore the tribe of Benjamin, securing wives for the survivors to rebuild their families and clans. But the Israelites were now forbidden by oath ever again to give their own daughters in marriage to that tribe. They remembered, however, that the town of Jabesh on the east side of the Jordan in Gilead had failed to send a delegation to Mizpah, and that the Jabeshites had not, therefore, subscribed to the oath. The penalty for such non-cooperation had been solemnly proclaimed to be death. So the Israelites sent an expedition of 10,000 men to destroy Jabesh and all of its inhabitants except for the unmarried women. In Jabesh there were 400 virgin girls, and these were given to the Benjaminite survivors. Since 200 more men still needed wives, the Israelite elders allowed them to lie in ambush in the vineyards of Shiloh during one of the great feasts and then dash out and carry away the girls of the dancing groups to be their wives.

When Israel Was without a Leader

During these years "everyone did whatever seemed to him to be the right thing" (Jgs 21:25). There was no leader to take Joshua's place. Waves of various alien tribes swept through the Promised Land, ravaging the countrysides and the people. Each tribe protected its possessions as well as it could, and often the neighboring tribes made common cause with it to repel the marauders. The Lord raised up temporary governors called "judges," who led the Israelites during these troubled times, literally rescuing the tribes from the threat of disastrous predicaments.

There were six "minor" judges, about whom very little has been recorded. The "major" judges rose to meet the challenges of great aggressors, when as yet "there was no king in Israel" (Jgs 21:25).

The Edomites, who had been left unscathed by the Hebrew armies of the exodus, now came marching into southern Canaan in the time of the judges. They were expelled by Othniel, Caleb's younger brother.

The Ammonites and Amalekites overran the old Amorite flat-lands of Reuben, Gad, and the half-tribe of Manasseh. They then crossed the Jordan and raided the highlands of Ephraim, Judah, and Benjamin. But Jephthah the Gileadite attacked their army from the rear and crushed the invaders. After this, however, the Ephraimites turned on Jephthah, who then denied them passage at the Jordan fords, slaying them if they failed to pronounce the password, "Shibboleth," without lisping.

Next, the Moabites moved troops into the area of Jericho. Ehud the Benjaminite removed this threat from Israel by plunging an eighteen-inch dagger into the belly of the grossly fat Moabite king and then leading the fighting force of Ephraim to a slaughter of the Moabite host.

Trouble later arose in central Palestine. Canaanite natives led by Sisera, army commander under the Canaanite federation, afflicted the Israelites for twenty years. Sisera boasted 900 iron-plated chariots. The prophetess Deborah marched with Barak the Naph-talite at the head of a column of 10,000 warriors from the tribes of Naphtali and Zebulon. They threw the enemy into confusion and won the battle of Tanaach-Megiddo, the date of which has been thought to be 1125 B.C. and which was memorable because it liberated the Jezreel Plain. Sisera met death at the hands of a woman, who drove a tent-peg through his temple with a mallet.

As we have seen, the period of the judges was marked by moral and religious disintegration. Many Israelites dishonored the Cove-nant they had made with the Lord. Intermarriage with the pagans became commonplace. The surname "Baal" was bestowed upon Israelite children, and shrines of the Baals were being built throughout the land. Even so, the ark and the Book of the Law in the tabernacle at Shiloh continued to be a rallying point for the twelve tribes, and from time to time a champion of God arose to remind them of the faith of their fathers. Such a one was Gideon in the day of the Midianite invasion.

Perhaps seeking to avenge the decimation of their people under Moses, the Midianites came swarming into Canaan accompanied by thousands of Amalekites—Bedouins riding out from the Arabian Desert, mounted on crescent-collared camels. In numbers past counting they ravaged the crops of the Hebrews all across the highlands and down toward Gaza, pillaging and foraging as they went. Gideon of Ophrah, a humble but valiant partisan of the Lord from the tribe of Manasseh, sounded the horn and rallied Manasseh, Asher, Zebulon, and the other northern tribes to do battle with this enemy. Out of the thousands who responded to Gideon's call, the Lord told Gideon to mobilize only 300 men so that when victory was achieved the Israelites would have to acknowledge that it was done by God's power and not their own.

Gideon proceeded to demoralize and rout the Midianites with a ruse. He then reassembled the thousands who had first volunteered, and set out in pursuit of the scattered Midianites and Amalekites, striking them down as they fled across the Jordan and up the valley of the Jabbok before they could reach safety in the eastern desert.

The final and longest-lasting threat to Israel came from the Philistines. The Philistines were not native to Canaan, but had invaded it from the west in the twelfth century B.C., one century after the invasion of the Hebrews from the east. Supported by ships standing out at sea, they had entrenched themselves by 1188 B.C. in the maritime towns of Gaza, Askelon, and Ashdod, and from these footholds had gone on to colonize the coastal plains, expanding into the foothills and valleys of the Israelite tribes of Dan and Judah. They brought with them the Iron Age and the horse, introducing iron-plated chariotry on a large scale, in addition to metal swords and shields. But they withheld and jealously guarded their knowledge of ironworking techniques from the Israelites.

We first encounter the Philistines in the Bible in the account of their conflict with Samson. Listed last among the judges, Samson was a strong man from the tribe of Dan born at Zorah in the upper Sorek Valley, "a nazirite from his mother's womb" (Jgs 13:5). As such, his hair had never been cut, and he had never drunk wine or strong drink. Before his birth an angel had predicted that he would be the one to "rescue Israel from the power of the Philistines" (Jgs 13:5). He never led a Hebrew tribe against the Philistines; rather, he was renowned as a man of prodigious strength who feuded with and downed the Philistines singlehandedly, killing thousands over a period of twenty years.

At Timnah in the rolling hills of the Shephelah, Samson slew and tore apart a lion with his bare hands. He later posed a riddle to the thirty Philistine men of his bridal party concerning the lion's carcass. His Philistine bride cajoled Samson into divulging the solution to the riddle, and then informed the bridegrooms of it. Samson was enraged. He descended to the seaside at Askelon and slew thirty Philistines, taking their robes in order to pay the wager he had lost in the matter of the riddle.

His marriage was then annulled by his wife's father. At this, Samson caught 300 foxes, tied blazing torches to their tails, and turned them loose to burn off the sheaves, shocks, vines, and olive trees of the Philistine countryside. He took refuge at the Rock of Etam and permitted himself to be bound with ropes by men of the tribe of Judah, who turned him over to the Philistines as a gesture of peace on their part. But when the Philistines came running toward him shouting triumphantly, he snapped his bonds, snatched up the jawbone of an ass, and with it slew a thousand of them. Almost dead from thirst after this massacre, Samson called upon the Lord and a spring of water gushed up in a hollow. He drank and was refreshed.

Later Samson went down to Gaza and visited with a harlot there. The natives surrounded the house where he was staying and set a watch at the town gate. At midnight Samson left his bed, made his way to the gate, and then broke it down, carrying it away on his shoulders—posts, bars, and all—all the way up to Hebron, which was about the highest point in Palestine.

Samson fell in love with a woman named Delilah who was in league with the chieftains of the Philistines. She pressed him to divulge the secret of his fabulous strength, and he gave her plausible, though untrue, answers three different times. At length, however, he foolishly revealed to Delilah the real source of his phenomenal strength: his head of hair. If his hair were ever cut he would be certain to lose his strength and become like any ordinary man. Delilah lulled Samson to sleep in her lap, and he awoke to find his locks sheared off. He was now too weak to fight off the Philistines who immediately leaped out from where they were hiding and assailed him. They gouged out his eyes, led him down to the prison at Gaza, and put him to work turning the prison's mill.

In time his hair grew out and his strength came back. At the high festival of the god Dagon he was brought to the temple to be made sport of by the multitude of Philistines who had assembled there. He was stationed, however, between the two main pillars that supported the temple structure. With a prayer to the Lord on his lips, Samson leaned hard against those pillars and pulled the building down upon them all, killing thousands more at the moment of his death than he had during his life.

CHAPTER EIGHT

SAMUEL

1 Samuel 1—8; 1 Chronicles 6:1–13

The Tabernacle at Shiloh

When Hanna, the barren wife of Elkanah, finally conceived and gave birth to Samuel at Ramah and turned the child over to the priest Eli at Shiloh to be raised in the service of the Lord, the Bible for the first time used the word "Temple" in reference to the tabernacle.

It was said that in those days the Lord did not often speak; yet he spoke to Samuel, calling out to him as he lay sleeping in the tabernacle near the ark. Still too young to understand whose voice was calling him, the lad was told by Eli to listen, for God was speaking to him. Eli insisted on knowing what the Lord had said to Samuel at those times. The youth fearfully complied: God had revealed to him that doom was about to fall on Eli's House because of his failure to reprimand his wayward and irreligious sons. As young Samuel grew to manhood, the Lord appeared to him often, and he was received as a prophet throughout Israel.

By that time, in its expansion Philistia had come to engulf nearly the whole of Dan and all of Judah's foothills. The Philistines had begun to pose a threat to the whole of Israel. In a great battle fought at Aphek within the border of Ephraim at about 1050 B.C., 4,000 Israelite warriors were left dead on the field. There was a pause in the fighting during which Israel brought the ark, in the company of Eli's sons, from Shiloh to the battlefield. The fighting resumed and ended in utter disaster for the Israelites: The Philistine chariots exacted a toll of 30,000 Israelite foot soldiers, the priest's sons were slain, and the ark was captured. When the news was brought to Shiloh that "the glory was gone from Israel" (1 Sm 4:22), the ninety-eight year old high priest Eli expired.

Confident now that the Israelites were bereft of their God, the Philistine victors carried the ark in triumph down to Ashdod in the Elah Valley near the sea, and set it up as a trophy of war next to the idol of their god Dagon. On successive mornings, however, they found the idol lying face down on the ground before the ark. On the second morning they found that its head and arms had been severed from its trunk, cluttering their temple's threshhold.

In the months that followed, the Philistines displayed the ark higher up the valley at Gath and across the foothills at Ekron. But they found that in every place to which the ark was taken a terrible pestilence broke out (which could well have been the bubonic plague). The Philistines became panic-stricken. They made gold casts both of the glandular swellings associated with the disease and of the rats thought to be its carriers. Placing these golden objects as guilt offerings in a box at the side of the ark, they mounted the ark and the box on a driverless cart and then made the cows harnessed to the cart bolt up a road toward Israel. Thus did they rid themselves of the odious symbol of triumph which had called down on them seven months of misfortune.

But the ark had been looted: Gone were the jar of manna and the sprouted branches. Only the two Tablets of the Law, which Moses had placed there at Mount Horeb, now remained.

Upon seeing the ark as it was being drawn by the lowing cows coming up the road from Philistia, the Hebrews who were harvesting wheat at Bethshemesh gave out a great shout of jubilation. They sacrificed the cows in thanksgiving to God and then sent messengers to the Gibeonite town of Kiriath-jearim, whose people came down and received the ark. They brought it to where it would repose for the next twenty years, on a hill twenty miles southeast of Shiloh in the house of Abinadab, with Eleazar, Abinadab's son, guarding it.

When Samuel had grown to manhood he made his home at Ramah, his birthplace, where he built an altar. The Israelites respected him as a prophet. They listened to him, and he was their judge, traveling a circuit every year that took him through Mizpah, Bethel, and Gilgal. He prevailed upon the people to give up their idols of Baal and Astarte, and he called a convocation of the tribes at Mizpah for a day of fasting and repentance.

The truculent Philistines, hearing that the Israelites were massed at Mizpah, came marching up against the place. By means of recurrent, mighty thunderstorms, however, the Lord threw them into such a panic that they fled in disorder. The Israelites pursued them and regained control of the outpost towns of Gath and Ekron in central Israel.

As the years passed it became clear that Samuel's two sons, like Eli's sons before him, were proving unprincipled and reprehensible. Though they were Samuel's deputies, they accepted bribes and perverted the administration of justice. This scandalous state of affairs brought popular discontent to a head, and a long-felt need that had been smoldering in the tribes now flared up. The Israelites wanted a more coherent national unity and a more stable form of government than the judges had been able to provide. So the elders of the tribes came together at Ramah and demanded that Samuel give them a king. In this they were following the example of the nations around them.

At first, Samuel was hostile to the idea, thinking that the people were rejecting their God as their only lord and king. He painted a dismal picture for them of what their life might come to be like under a king's rule. Their sons would be put to manufacturing weapons for the royal arsenal or drafted into the king's military service. Their daughters would be taken as maids into the royal household. The people's lands and crops would be severely tithed to support the government. Nevertheless, they insisted, "We want a king to rule us, such as other nations have, a king who will lead us in warfare and fight our battles" (1 Sm 3:20). The Lord bade Samuel to listen to the voice of the people. Although they were rejecting direct divine rule, God's rule could still persist under a king who would be anointed by the Lord as his delegated representative.

CHAPTER NINE

SAUL

1 Samuel 8:29–34; 9; 10; 31; 1 Chronicles 9:35–44; 10:1–14

The First King of Israel

The Lord told Samuel he would send him a man from the land of Benjamin who was to be anointed king of Israel. This man was Saul, the tall and handsome son of Kish. Kish had just sent Saul from their home at Gibeah in search of some animals that had wandered off. On his way through the countryside Saul happened to come up to the town gate of Ramah just as Samuel was going out to the high place and the altar he had built on it. As he looked at Saul, Samuel heard the Lord say, "That is the man!" (1 Sm 9:17). So he took Saul along with him to the hilltop and offered a sacrifice to God. Afterward, Samuel seated him at the head of the thirty guests he had invited to the sacrificial meal, and made sure that Saul received the choicest portion to eat.

They returned to Samuel's house, and Samuel laid a mattress on his rooftop for Saul to pass the night. At daybreak the two of them rose and walked out to the edge of town. Samuel paused there and poured a vial of oil on Saul's head, and kissed him. "You are the man the Lord has anointed to rule over his people and save them from the enemies that surround them" (1 Sm 10:1). Samuel predicted that the spirit of God would come upon Saul. And as Saul approached Gibeah, the young man met and joined a group of prophets who were descending from the high place to the strains of harp, tambourine, flute, and lyre. Though this all came to pass, Saul said nothing about his consecration when he arrived home.

Samuel called for a meeting of all the tribes at Mizpah in order to choose by lot the king they had asked the Lord to give them. Of the twelve tribes the lot fell to Benjamin; within that tribe, it fell to the clan of Matri; and within that clan, to Saul the son of Kish. But Saul was nowhere to be seen; he was hiding among the baggage. Samuel had him brought forward and presented him to the assembly, a man in his prime, standing head and shoulders taller than all others. At that, the cry rang out from the crowd, "Long live the king!" (1 Sm 10:24). When Saul went home, a sworn elite went with him to be his guard. These events took place at about 1020 B.C.

A month later the Ammonites laid siege to Jabesh-gilead. The inhabitants offered to surrender, but the Ammonites refused to let them do so unless they would agree to let their right eyes be gouged out. News of this was brought to Saul at Gibeah. In a towering rage Saul butchered his yoke of oxen, cut them up in pieces, and sent a part to each of the tribes. He threatened to do the same to the oxen of any man who failed to join him in fighting against the Ammonites.

The tribes responded in force by volunteering 330,000 men, and Saul sent encouragement to Jabesh-gilead that help was on the way. He split his army into three divisions, hurled them across the Jordan, and slaughtered the Ammonites mercilessly until noon. In honor of God for granting this victory, Saul tempered his fury by allowing the Ammonites he captured to remain alive.

The Israelite army moved to Gilgal, where Saul was proclaimed king and peace offerings were made. Samuel addressed the tribes, saying, "If both you and the king who rules you follow the Lord your God, all will go well with you" (1 Sm 12:14). Except for a small standing contingent of 2,000 soldiers whom he kept with him at Michmash, and another contingent of 1,000 under his son Jonathan's command several miles away at Geba, Saul disbanded the troops, letting the men return home. In view of what was about to happen, this was probably not wise.

Saul Falls from God's Favor

The Israelites now rose up against their Philistine oppressors. Jonathan son of Saul smashed the Philistine post at Gibeah. Saul had the trumpets sounded throughout Israel as a signal that the revolt was under way. The Hebrew tribes massed at Gilgal, near the Jordan, while the Philistines rapidly ascended the hill country with 3,000 chariots and numerous infantry. The Philistines occupied the pass at Michmash, overlooking the lower Jordan and commanding the Gilgal lowland. Down below, Saul and Jonathan were waiting impatiently for Samuel to arrive and offer sacrifice. The situation of the Hebrews grew desperate: The enemy was taking control of the heart of their southern highlands, while they themselves were lying idle in a strategically poor position. During the week of waiting, Saul's army was gradually melting away as soldiers deserted.

When the seventh day came and went and Samuel still did not come, the king took matters into his own hands and offered up the holocaust himself. Samuel arrived soon afterward and berated Saul for "playing the fool" (1 Sm 13:13). Saul should not have offered the sacrifice on his own initiative. Samuel now prophesied that the kingship would pass from Saul and his House.

With their sadly depleted ranks Saul and Jonathan managed to get to the flank of the Philistine encampment, stationing themselves just a few miles away on the eminence of Geba. The Philistines were confident that they had the Hebrews at their mercy. However, they made a serious tactical error by splitting their strength into three columns which fanned out in order to scour and lay waste the country. One column went north, and another south; the main holding force headed westward toward Philistia.

Jonathan then made a daring foray. Without revealing his plan to anyone, he set out with his armor-bearer to surprise the enemy outpost at the pass. They climbed up on one of the spurs in the pass and allowed the Philistine sentinels to see them. When the sentinels dared them to advance, they swooped down and killed twenty of the enemy. The Philistines in the main camp saw their advance guard falling back and became panic-stricken.

At Geba the Israelite lookout could see that the enemy's camp was breaking up and, to find out who was doing the fighting, Saul called the roll. He discovered that it was Jonathan and his armor-bearer who were missing. Saul's 600, aided by deserters returning to the ranks, then rushed to Jonathan's side and turned the attack into a Philistine rout. The enemy was driven back eight miles west down to Beth-horon and out of the southern highlands.

To follow up this victory and to obtain the Lord's blessing for a still greater victory, Saul ordered a fast to be observed by all. No one was to take food until sunset the next day. The following morning they fought the Philistines all the way back to the valley of the Aijalon, and at the end of the day the wearied warriors were all famished. Each man slaughtered an ox or a sheep from the booty that had been taken, but ate the meat without having drained it of its blood. In so doing they violated the Law. Jonathan, too, had done wrong: Unaware of his father's injunction to fast, he had eaten from a honeycomb. Only after he had eaten was he told of the king's order.

Saul decided to press the fight and go down under cover of darkness to pursue, slay, and plunder until dawn. But when the priest besought the Lord for his help and blessing, he received no answer. Evil had been done in the Lord's sight.

Saul then went to stand in front of his troops with Jonathan at his side. He swore that whoever had sinned and thus brought upon Israel the Lord's displeasure—even if it were his own son— would be put to death. Lots were cast, the first indicating that the ritual fault of the soldiers was not being held against them. The second marked Jonathan as the one who was guilty. Jonathan confessed to his thoughtless transgression, and declared himself ready to die if his father's oath required it. Saul was, in fact, about to carry out the execution, but his troops would not abide it. They had seen Jonathan perform exploits that day which could only have been achieved with the help of God. So Saul was forced to reprieve his son, and in consequence of the incident decided against making further pursuit of the Philistines.

Saul made no pretense of grandeur. He ruled his kingdom from a diminutive throne room in an unassuming state house in Gibeah, the old and tragic Benjaminite capital. He was surrounded by his three sons, of whom Jonathan was the eldest, and by two daughters, of whom the younger was named Michal. He was always on the watch for strong and valiant recruits for service under his uncle Abner, who commanded the army and with whom he was often in the field. He had humbled the Philistines and staved off the threat that they presented from the west, and later he had repelled thrusts coming from the east and south.

Farther south, however, the Amalekites were still living secure and unmolested in the Negeb. But the Lord had vowed, "I shall wipe out the memory of Amalek from the earth!" (Ex 17:14). And Moses had stated, "The Lord is at war with Amalek from age to age" (Ex 17:16). Now, two centuries later, the time had come for the wreaking of the divine vengeance. Through Samuel God now bade Saul to wipe the Amalekites from the earth. They were to be put under the ban—which meant death to them and every living thing among them.

At Telaim Saul reviewed his soldiers, of whom there were 210,000. Then he laid an ambush in a dry wadi some distance in front of the Amalekite stronghold. From there Saul sent word secretly to the Kenites, a people who had been friendly to the Hebrews at the time of the exodus, but were now living with the Amalekites. Saul told them that if they left the city their lives would be spared. The Israelites then fell upon the Amalekite stronghold and took it, going on to ravage the land as far as the Shur wilderness and the frontier of Egypt. But Saul made the mistake of letting their king, Agag, live, and of sparing the best of the Amalekite herds and flocks, thus violating the ban. His excuse was that he was saving them for holocausts at Gilgal. When the prophet Samuel heard the bleating of the sheep and the lowing of the oxen and spied the Amalekite king, he asked Saul:

Does the Lord take pleasure in holocausts and sacrifices more than in obedience to his will? Because you have not fulfilled the commission laid upon you, God regrets having made you king over Israel. He is going to tear the kingdom from your hands and give it to someone else more worthy than you. (1 Sm 15:22–3, 28).

Then Samuel himself slew the Amalekite king. Saul had done what he did in order to cultivate good will among his troops. Acknowledging that he had sinned, he clutched the hem of Samuel's robe, begging for forgiveness. It was all to no avail, except that the prophet did consent to accompany him to Gilgal so that he would not lose face before the elders and the people.

CHAPTER TEN

DAVID

Ruth; 1 Samuel 16—30; 2 Samuel; 1 Kings 1;
2; 1 Chronicles 2:9–17; 3:1–9; 5:27–41;
6:1–66; 9:10–34; 11—29; 2 Chronicles
1:1–6; Psalms 3, 7, 8, 18, 34, 51, 52, 54,
56, 57, 58, 60, 63, 72, 96, 105, 106, 142;
Ecclesiasticus 47:2–12

A Boy Fells a Giant

The Lord reproved Samuel for grieving so much at Saul's fall from grace. Samuel was then directed to fill a horn with oil and go to Bethlehem to the sheepherder Jesse, for it would be from among the sons of Jesse that Israel's new king was to be chosen. Samuel took a heifer with him for a sacrificial offering and meal to which he invited Jesse and his family and eight sons.

Jesse was an Ephrathite of Bethlehem in Judah, and a grandson of the Moabite Ruth. Ruth was the widow of a man of Judah; her subsequent marriage to Boaz was the union from which Jesse's father, Obed, had been born.

When Samuel arrived at Jesse's house, Jesse presented to Samuel all of his sons except the youngest, who was out tending the sheep in the pasture. Samuel insisted on sending for him, too, before they sat down to eat. The eldest son, Eliab, was tall and especially handsome, and Samuel thought that he would surely be the man selected by God. The Lord, who looks at the heart, chose the youngest one, however: "Anoint him. He is the one!" (1 Sm

16:12). So Samuel anointed the boy, and the spirit of God descended on him.

Three stories about young David are inserted into the biblical narrative at this point. One story indicates that Saul, without knowing who David was, arranged for him to serve at the royal court by playing his harp to cheer him up whenever he felt depressed. The second tradition records that Saul, upon seeing that David was brave, prudent, and influential, made him his armor-bearer.

The third story is that of the confrontation of David and Goliath. The Philistines had marched up again into Israel's hill country, and the opposing armies were drawn up facing each other on the two sides of the Valley of the Terebinth. Jesse's three oldest sons were in the king's service, and David was sent to bring them some roasted grain and loaves of bread, and bring their commanding officer ten cheeses.

The Philistines had a mighty warrior who daily shamed the Hebrews. He taunted them to send out someone to fight him in single combat and thereby decide the conflict. But not even the bravest Israelite dared accept that challenge. For this Philistine was a giant—nine feet nine inches tall—who wore battle gear that must have weighed 300 pounds. His name was Goliath, and his home was the town of Gath, only twelve miles from the Sorek Valley which had been the home of an earlier strong man, Samson.

David was convinced that he could fell Goliath and so erase the shame of Israel. He found out from the soldiers that the reward for doing so would be great riches from the royal treasury, the king's younger daughter in marriage, and the freedom of all Israel to his father's family. Despite a reproof from his brother Eliab, David went to Saul and offered to fight Goliath. Saul warned him he was only a youth, whereas Goliath was a seasoned warrior, but David boasted that he had killed lions and bears preying on his father's sheep. He could just as easily bring down this mammoth braggart who daily defied the Hebrew army, he said. So Saul presented the lad with his own armor of breastplate and sword, but David found it too heavy and took it off. He went forth to face Goliath with only his shepherd's staff and slingshot.

When the Philistine saw David he roared his contempt and heaped scorn on the young Hebrew. "Am I a dog to be come at with a stick?" he growled (1 Sm 17:43). But David shouted in return, "I come against you in the name of the Lord of hosts, the God of Israel's armies, to cut off your head and give your carcass to the birds and beasts" (1 Sm 17:45–46). Then David fitted a stone to his sling, drew his arm back, and let fly. The stone struck Goliath on the forehead with a force that crushed his skull, and he toppled to the ground. In an instant David had the giant's sword out of its scabbard and with it severed his neck. The Philistine army took flight, and the Hebrews followed in a far-ranging pursuit. David carried away Goliath's head and armor as trophies of his victory.

The news of this extraordinary exploit done by an unknown youth reverberated throughout the land of Israel. Through it David won the favor of Saul. He was put in charge of one of the fighting contingents and, because of his ability as a soldier, he rapidly rose in the esteem of both ranks and officers. So meteoric, in fact, was the young man's rise in popular esteem that Saul began to take umbrage at him as a potential contender for the throne. When returning from the scene of a routing of the Philistines, Saul and David were greeted by the girls of the towns, who came out dancing to the sound of tambourine and lyre. They sang, "Saul has slain his thousands, David his tens of thousands!" (1 Sm 18:7).

While distrust and dislike crept into the heart of the king, Saul's son Jonathan, on the contrary, felt drawn to David and became strongly attached to him. They made a pact of friendship together, and Jonathan gave David his cloak, armor, belt, sword, and bow.

The King's Hatred of David

Saul now made David commander of a thousand in the hopes that he would be cut down by a Philistine sword. When the princess Michal fell in love with David, Saul let it be known that he would give her to David in marriage if he would bring the king proof that he had killed a hundred Philistines. David brought him proof of 200 dead. Saul then gave David his daughter Michal for his wife, and David dwelt with her in Gibeah.

Though Saul had no way of knowing that Samuel had anointed David as his successor, his heart rankled at the repeated successes and growing popularity of his son-in-law. This thought became an obsession with him. One day, while David was playing the harp for Saul, the king suddenly hurled his spear at him. David dodged the throw and sped from the court. That night the king sent agents to the young man's house with orders to dispatch him; but Michal warned him of what was going on. "If you do not get away tonight, you will be a dead man" (1 Sm 19:11). He escaped through a window.

David went to Ramah and lived with Samuel in the huts of the prophets. Though Saul came after him there, David again got away. Later, Jonathan came out to him, and David confessed what a dangerous pass things had come to between him and the king. "There is now but a step between me and death" (1 Sm 20:3). Jonathan promised to find out the true state of his father's mind with regard to David.

This was the time of the feast of the new moon. When the second day of the feast went by without David being present at the royal table, Saul exploded in anger at David's patent avoidance of him. Filled with fear and hatred he berated Jonathan with the words, "As long as that son of Jesse is alive, you cannot make good your own claim to the kingship." Then he added what he really had in mind. "You shall send for him and bring him to me. For he is doomed to die!" (1 Sm 20:31). The king met Jonathan's protest with a brandishing of his spear. The next morning the prince went to the field where David was hiding and informed him of the king's intentions. At this, David fled to Nob, a city only a few miles southeast of Gibeah and where the tabernacle was now located.

At Nob David was provided with five loaves of consecrated showbread—bread usually reserved only to the priests—and the huge sword he had taken from Goliath. He then went on to Gath, the former home of Goliath, but he soon found out that he, a lone Hebrew, was unwelcome there. He was even suspected of being the Hebrew prince celebrated in the song, "Saul has slain his thousands, David his tens of thousands" (1 Sm 18:7). To extricate himself from this peril, David pretended to be a madman and made himself a nuisance by drumming on the doors of houses, with spittle drooling down his beard. Finally, the chieftain would no longer abide his presence in the town. David left and took shelter in a cave in the area of the Rock of Adullam, a little above the undulating lowland of the Shepelah and about twelve miles from Hebron and his home, Bethlehem. There his brothers and his father's family came to join him, as well as 400 others, mostly outlaws, who rallied round him.

David transported his father and mother beyond the reach of the vengeful power of Saul to the country of Moab, east of the Dead Sea. As we remember, David's great grandmother Ruth was a Moabite. David now left his parents in the care of the king of Moab. Then at the counsel of the prophet Gad, who was to remain David's prophet throughout his life, he made his way back to the land of Judah.

Meanwhile, from where he sat under the tamarisk on the high place of Gibeah, Saul was inveighing openly against Jonathan for his disloyalty. Seizing this chance to ingratiate himself with the king, Doeg the Edomite informed Saul that he had been present at Nob when the priests had befriended David and consulted the Lord for him. Saul was infuriated. He sent for the high priest Ahimelech and his family and commanded that they all be put to the sword. Since the king's guard refused to put the priests to death the Edomite slew them himself. Abiathar, a son of the high priest, was the only one who managed to escape the massacre. He went to David and told him what had happened. Abiathar remained with him and served him as his priest for the rest of David's life.

Not long afterward, David heard that the Philistines were attacking the town of Keilah, four miles southeast of Adullam. After consulting the Lord he swept down with his men and beat off the besiegers. To Saul's way of thinking, David was now caught in a trap of his own making. Saul set out immediately to attack him, but David, ever alert, had already departed for the higher altitude of the wilderness of Ziph, located in the eastern highlands sloping down to the Dead Sea. His followers at that time numbered about 600.

Here in the region below Hebron and Carmel, in the clefts and hollows above the Dead Sea, the drama of Saul's unrelenting pursuit and David's hairbreadth bolts away from capture was about to be played out. Jonathan went to find David at Horesh. Though he was himself the royal heir, Jonathan willingly gave up the throne to his friend. The two of them then reaffirmed their brotherhood pact. After Jonathan's visit, some of the inhabitants of Ziph came to Saul and offered to betray David in his hide-out at Horesh on the hill of Hachilah. But David moved on up into the wilderness of Maon, just south of Carmel. There Saul came in hot and deadly pursuit, he and his force moving along one side of a rocky gorge while David and his troops scurried along the opposite side, desperately striving not to be outflanked. Critical as the situation was, it was saved for David by word that the Philistines had invaded Israel again, necessitating Saul's breaking off the chase.

David seized this opportunity to descend the eastern slopes of the highlands all the way down to the shore of the Dead Sea at Engedi, a region in which places of concealment abounded. Saul, having chased the Philistines back to their own country, resumed the hunt for his son-in-law, coming back this time with 3,000 picked men.

In the course of the search the king withdrew into a cave to relieve himself, unaware that David and his men were there in that same cave. David noiselessly came up behind Saul and stealthily cut off a border of the royal mantle with his sword. After the king had issued from the cave, David called out to him, "I hold the border of your mantle in my hand—I could have killed you. But even though you are hunting me down to take my life, there is neither malice nor treason in my mind" (1 Sm 24:12). Saul could not help but thank him for having spared his life. Seeming to have known that David was destined to become king of Israel, he begged him to show mercy to the present royal House. David accepted Saul's apology, but cautiously returned to the wilderness of Maon.

There was a wealthy sheep raiser of Carmel named Nabal who churlishly refused to show any gratitude or hospitality toward David's men, even though they had guarded his holdings for him in the wasteland. This made David angry, and he started out for

Carmel with some of his troops, intending to chasten Nabal. Nabal's wife, Abigail, heard that David would be coming in force, and set out without a word to her husband to placate David and apologize for her husband's behavior. As she came up from behind a spur of the mountain, David and his detachment suddenly appeared before her. Abigail dismounted and bowed before him, taking upon herself the blame for her husband's insensitivity and rudeness. She finished by lauding David for fighting the battles of the Lord. Appeased and impressed by her words, David gave thanks to God for sending this woman to forestall the bloodshed he had contemplated. He accepted the gifts she had brought him and his men, and sent her back home in peace.

Nabal died mysteriously ten days later. David, who had been struck by Abigail's graciousness, sent her an offer of marriage which she readily accepted. She thus became the second of his two wives; for Saul had taken Michal back and given her to another man, while David had married Ahinoam of Jezreel.

Inconstant as ever, Saul now had second thoughts about his reconciliation with David. He renewed his search for David, knowing that his quarry was again living in the barrens of Ziph. The king gathered 3,000 of his men and bivouacked along the road at the hill of Hachilah. News of his coming had been brought to David, who went to a spot that overlooked Saul's camp in order to observe it. He asked those who were with him if there was anyone among them who would volunteer to go down with him to penetrate the post after darkness fell, and his nephew Abishai at once stepped forward.

That night the two of them stealthily made their way through the enemy camp past Abner to where Saul was sleeping. The king's spear was stuck in the ground next to his head. Abishai whispered that if David so desired he would transfix Saul to the ground with the king's own spear. David would not permit it, however. Instead, they merely appropriated Saul's spear and canteen and carried these off without awakening anyone.

At first light, from the mountain top on the other side of the valley David shouted down to Abner, "You deserve death for failure to guard your lord! Look for the king's spear and the canteen that was at his head" (1 Sm 26:16). He called upon Saul to send up a man to retrieve the spear. Then he shouted:

> The king of Israel has come out to seek my life as if he were hunting partridge in the mountains. Today the Lord delivered you into my power, but because you are God's anointed I would not lift a hand against you. (1 Sm 26:20,23)

Saul, addressing him now as "my son David, who respected my life today" (1 Sm 26:21), admitted his guilt and protested that he would do David no further harm.

David Becomes a Soldier of Fortune

It was clear, however, that Saul was not to be trusted. Since David could not hope by simple wiliness to escape the king forever, he sought safety at Gath among the Philistines. He appeared boldly before Achish, the king, and applied for possession of an outlying Philistine settlement where he could serve Achish as his vassal. Ziklag, a settlement just west of the land of Judah and north of the Negeb, was given him for his headquarters.

At Ziklag a number of Hebrew men of valor, famous for their ability as soldiers, joined themselves to David. Among them were twenty-three Benjaminites, kinsmen of Saul—a group that included Ishmaiah from Gibeon, who was to make such a name for himself as to eventually become the leader of the elite corps of the Thirty. Eleven Gadite officers also came to David at this time— men who had the look of lions and the speed of gazelles and were all unusually proficient in the use of spear and shield. All of them had been in command of contingents either of a hundred or a thousand. There were other Benjaminites, too, as well as men of Judah who came to swell the Israelite force at Ziklag. When David welcomed them, bidding them before God to be true to his cause, Amasai, who was destined one day to become a leader of the Thirty, reassured him of their loyalty.

For the next sixteen months and more, David earned the favor of the Philistines by policing the neighboring deserts to the south and southwest. He conducted repeated forays against the tribes that inhabited the Shur wilderness and the land bordering on Egypt. During this entire time, David cleverly misled Achish into thinking that his raiding was directed against the Negeb of Judah and the Kenites, while in fact he was actually relieving the Negeb of pressure from the Geshurites, Girzites, and Amalekites. David would dutifully bring back the booty of sheep, oxen, donkeys, camels, and garments, but he was careful never to bring back any captives who might betray the true source of this spoil. Therefore, while he was rising ever higher in favor with his kinsmen in Judah, his Philistine lord imagined that the opposite was true.

At any rate, David was now inextricably entangled in the fortunes of Philistia, and the Philistine nation was at that time preparing for all-out war upon the Israelite nation. Achish assumed that David and his Hebrew band would, as loyal vassals, join forces with him; he even appointed them his personal guard. The army of the Philistines rendezvoused at Shunem on the Plain of Jezreel. The tribes of Israel mustered at Gilboa, a nearby spur running down from the highlands.

King Saul, terrified at the prospect of a head-on collision of the armies, was at a loss where to turn for a source of divine guidance. The prophet Samuel had passed away, and the Lord would give Saul no reply through dream, oracle, or prophecy. Saul was at his wit's end. Finally, he learned that there was a witch in the town of En-dor who had the ability to consult the spirits of the dead. Saul decided to go to her and make her raise the spirit of Samuel, so that he could ask advice from him.

Saul did so, and Samuel appeared to him as the ghost of an old man risen out of the earth wrapped in his mantle. He told Saul that the Lord had abandoned him for his disobedience in the matter of Amalek and was now with David his neighbor. Furthermore, he said that Saul would be defeated in battle the next day and that he and his sons would pass from the land of the living into the realm of the shades. Saul, who had eaten and drunk nothing all that day and night, fell down in a dead faint. When he revived, he ate a little food and returned disconsolate to the Israelite camp.

On their way up to Shunem the Philistine officers had reviewed their forces at Aphek, the site of the battle in which the ark had been captured some years before. When the Philistine commanders saw David and his Hebrew contingent, they objected to Achish that these men were of the enemy's blood and therefore not to be trusted—in the thick of the fighting they might switch sides. So Achish told David to go back to Ziklag. David objected strenuously, though secretly he was no doubt relieved, even elated, at not being called upon to fight against his kinsmen. During the three-days' march back to Ziklag, seven officers from the half-tribe of Manasseh came to join David's company. When they all arrived back at Ziklag, however, they found that the city had been stormed and burned to the ground in their absence by the Amalekites. The raiders had also carried off the Hebrews' women and children.

The men's grief and resentment at the loss of their families stirred them to consider stoning David. In this crisis David calmly called upon his priest Abiathar to consult the Lord. The oracle directed them to set out with their leader in lightning pursuit of the Amalekites.

At this, all thought of stoning David was abandoned. He rallied his men and set off with such haste that by the time they reached the Wadi Besor, 200 of his men were exhausted and had to be left there to guard the baggage. As they continued their pursuit, David and the 400 men who remained with him came across a sick and famished Egyptian slave whom the Amalekites had abandoned in the wilderness three days before. He told David where the marauders were heading.

Blowing in upon the Amalekites like a desert wind, the pursuers found and took them unawares. They were scattered about, eating and drinking to celebrate the good fortune they had had in their raid. David's men cut the Amalekites to pieces, but 400 of them managed to mount camels and get away. The Israelite families were all recovered unharmed and, in addition to the property and possessions that had been seized at Ziklag, the avengers now had the Amalekite livestock to drive back to their ravaged settlement. Out of this spoil David made gifts to the elders of Hebron and a dozen other towns just south of that city. By doing this he was wisely cultivating favor in his native land of Judah.

At Saul's Death David Starts to Reign

The battle of which Saul was so much in dread did in fact take place at Mount Gilboa, and the Hebrews were roundly defeated. Saul died on the field, together with Jonathan and two other sons. One account of Saul's death reports that the king, knowing the battle was lost, had killed himself by falling upon his sword after being mortally wounded by an arrow. Another tradition tells that he had told an Amalekite soldier to strike him down because he was being so hard pressed by the enemy that he lacked the strength to continue resisting. This soldier had come to David with Saul's crown and bracelet, expecting to be rewarded, but David had him executed on the spot for daring to slay the Lord's Anointed.

In any case, it is clear that the Israelites in the army had fled, and that those in the nearby towns had also abandoned the fight. The Philistines now dominated the northern highlands, leaving Israel in control of only those lands lying on the far side of the Jordan. The day after the battle, while stripping the dead for valuables, the Philistines found the bodies of Saul and his sons. They cut off Saul's head and took his armor, and then exhibited these as trophies throughout the towns of Philistia. Finally, they nailed up his head in the temple of Dagon, put his armor on display in the temple of Astarte, and hung his body together with the bodies of his sons on the wall of Beth-shan, overlooking the lowlands of the Jordan Valley.

The citizens of Jabesh in the Gilead lowland, the town which Saul had delivered from the Ammonites, made a night march to Beth-shan, retrieved the corpses of the king and his sons, and, after cremating them, buried their bones at Jabesh.

This inglorious end to Saul's reign cannot obscure all the glory that he had, in fact, won. He had fought Israel's enemies everywhere—Moabites, Ammonites, Edomites, even the west Aramaeans. He had delivered Israel from the plundering of the Amalekites, and he had died bravely battling the Philistines.

All Israel, and especially David, mourned for Saul and Jonathan. David lamented:

O mountains of Gilboa, may no rain or dew fall on you. O
daughters of Israel, weep for Saul. How the heroes have fallen
in the thick of battle, slain upon the heights. O Jonathan, I
grieve for you, my brother. Dear to me were you, and your love
more wonderful than a woman's. (2 Sm 1:21, 24–26)

The Lord then told David to go up to Hebron with his wives
and followers. David's past efforts to gain the support and loyalty
of the people of Judah now bore fruit: His many partisans from
his native tribe gathered en masse to anoint him as Judah's king.
The time was then about 1000 B.C., and he had just reached the age
of thirty.

This action, however, was bound to stir up trouble among the
other tribes. For example, the tribe of Benjamin had, during the
reign of the Benjaminite Saul, enjoyed the fealty of all the other
tribes and hence would be loathe to relinquish that honor. It was
well known that David meant to claim the loyalty of all Israel,
for in sending thanks to the citizens of Jabesh-gilead for the solic-
itude they showed in giving Saul burial, he had also invited
their support.

Abner, the commander of the Israelite army under Saul, had
installed Saul's surviving son, Ishbaal, upon the throne at Mahanaim in Gilead. From Mahanaim, Abner marched into the southern
highlands and met David's fighting force at Gibeon, six miles
northwest of Jerusalem. David had left his troops in the charge of
the three sons of his sister Zeruiah, namely, Joab, Abishai, and
Asahel. Of these three, Abishai, who had been with David in the
wilderness of Ziph, was the eldest, and Asahel the youngest, but
Joab had been appointed commander of the army.

The two armies deployed on opposite sides of the Pool of
Gibeon. Abner suggested, and Joab agreed, that a dozen combatants from each side should decide the conflict. After they had
fought, however, all twenty-four of them lay dead. In the full
battle that ensued, the men of Judah prevailed, forcing their foe
to retreat.

In the pursuit, Asahel singled out Abner and ran ahead of his
comrades, hoping to vanquish the enemy commander. Abner entreated him to cease his chase, but Asahel refused. So Abner side-

stepped, and speared him through the waist. This caused a momentary lull in the fighting. Then Joab and Abishai drove Abner to a hilltop, but the Benjaminites rallied round their leader in close formation to protect him. Abner asked for a truce, and Joab had the trumpet sounded to halt the attack. Abner then withdrew from the field and crossed over the Jordan to Mahanaim. He had lost 360 men; Joab had lost only twenty. By this time the sun had set, and by marching through the night, Joab reached Hebron at dawn. On the way he buried Asahel at Bethlehem.

During this period David acquired a total of six wives, and he had a son born to him by each of them. The first of these six sons was Amnon, born of Ahinoam of Jezreel; the second was Chileab, born of Abigail; the third was Absalom, born of Maacah, daughter of the sovereign of Geshur on the eastern side of the Sea of Galilee; the fourth was Adonijah, born of Haggith; the fifth was Shephatiah, born of Abital; and the sixth, Itream, of Eglah.

Meanwhile, Abner had become the de facto ruler of the House of Saul, and over Ishbaal's mild protestation he had even taken one of Saul's concubines for his wife. In time he became convinced that the throne of all Israel rightfully belonged to David, and the other tribes agreed with him.

So Abner went with twenty of his men to Hebron to make peace with David. David was open to negotiations, but he did stipulate one condition: the return of Michal, his former wife, to him. Abner complied, and David held a feast for him and his twenty companions. Then Abner left, intending to convoke the tribes and so gain formal consent from them to transfer their allegiance to David.

Scarcely had he left, however, when Joab turned up at Hebron with the army and inveighed against Abner as being full of deceit and evil designs. Without David's knowledge Joab sent messengers to intercept Abner and bring him back to Hebron. Abner returned and met Joab at the town gate, and Joab stabbed him to death in retaliation for the death of his brother Asahel.

David mourned Abner's death greatly. He called down upon Joab's House curses of leprosy, enervation, and death by sword or famine. He praised Abner as having been a prince of Israel and he made the soldiers rend their cloaks and don sackcloth. David wept at Abner's grave and went without food until sundown.

But now two of Ishbaal's chieftains slew Ishbaal while he was sleeping in his house. They raced to lay Ishbaal's head at the feet of David, expecting him to reward them. David did not react that way.

> The man who thought he was bringing me good news when he told me Saul was dead—that man I seized and had killed at Ziklag, rewarding him thus for his "good news." How much more now when evil men have slain an honest man in his bed, am I bound to hold you responsible for his death and wipe you from the earth? (2 Sm 4:10–11)

Then he ordered his soldiers to put the murderers to death and hang them up beside the pool at Hebron with their hands and feet cut off. And he had the head of Ishbaal buried in Abner's grave.

When David had reigned seven and a half years as king of Judah, he was made king of all Israel by acclamation. This was when he was in his late thirties, at about 992 B.C. Rallying to him at Hebron to join Judah's 6,300 men-at-arms came some 332,800 troops from the eleven other tribes. Simultaneously provisions from all parts of Israel converged on Hebron: trains of asses, mules, oxen, and camels. These were all laden with flour cakes, pressed figs, clusters of raisins, skins of wine, and horns of oil. Also in the caravans were herds of cattle and sheep. David drew up a pact with the elders, and they, in keeping with what the Lord had enjoined upon the prophet Samuel, anointed him their king. For three days David kept festival and dined with the throng. Great was the joy in Israel. As many of 18,000 criers were dispatched throughout the land of the Hebrews to proclaim that David's reign had begun.

News of the inauguration shook the complacency of Philistia, which interpreted the event as a signal of Hebrew rebellion. So the Philistines came marching up to destroy the new sovereign and his kingdom. They encamped in the Rephaim Valley, a few miles below the Bethlehem height. David prepared to confront and attack their expedition. He established his headquarters at Adullam, and while he was there he was treated to a spectacular show of devotion when three of his men proved they were willing to go to any length to satisfy his slightest need or desire.

These men had overheard him sighing, "Oh, that I could have a drink of water from the well at the gate of Bethlehem!" (2 Sm 23:15). Although Bethlehem was held by the Philistines those three valiants of the corps known as the "Thirty" burst through the Philistine camp and climbed the eleven miles to the Bethlehem height. They gladly risked their lives in order to draw a cup of water from that well at the gate and bring it to him. Overcome by this gesture, David refused to drink the water. "God forbid that I drink the blood of those brave fellows, who got this at the peril their lives!" (2 Sm 23:16–17). And he poured the cup out on the ground as an offering to the Lord.

David threw his column against the expeditionary force of the Philistine line, dispersing their ranks and gathering up the idols they left behind in their flight. The Philistines regrouped and deployed in the Rephaim Valley. The Lord told David to go behind the enemy opposite some balsam trees and to attack when the wind in the tree tops made a sound like marching footsteps. David obeyed, and aided by the element of surprise he drove the invaders out of Israel all the way back to Gezer and the seaboard, where they had been entrenched for generations.

Thus did the "revolt" of the Hebrews end in a signal victory for them. The Philistines had lost their hold on Israel, never again to regain it in the time of David.

Jerusalem

The new kingdom needed a new capital, one militarily stronger and politically better located than the town of Hebron. It was clear that the stronghold of Jebus—eighteen miles to the north of Hebron, still in the highlands, but a quarter of a mile lower in altitude—would be ideal for the purpose, since it was situated midway between the northern and southern tribes.

Although Jebus had never been successfully assaulted David decided that he must and would take it. He prepared a siege, knowing that the steep-walled valleys on its southern and eastern sides constituted a truly formidable defense. The city had been called Jerusalem in Abraham's day, but had come to be known as Jebus from the name of the people who dwelt there before and during the time of Joshua and the judges. The walls of the city enclosed a low mountain—Mount Zion—which bulged up from a rocky plateau. This plateau was the top of a bluff that loomed fifty to sixty feet above a pair of converging valleys. The Jebusites boasted that their city was impregnable and could be defended even by cripples.

Yet there was a point at which its defense was vulnerable. The ancient inhabitants of this stronghold had bored a fifty-foot vertical shaft down through the rock to the ceiling of a cavern with a spring-fed pool. Access to the shaft was by a rock-hewn, sloping passageway from just inside the city's eastern wall. The purpose of this was to secure safe access to water in time of siege. But if buckets could be dropped through the shaft and into the pool, a brave soldier could go up through the same shaft and penetrate the defense of the city. David offered a reward to anyone who would do this.

Joab, followed by others, accepted this challenge and delivered the city into David's hands. Afterward, David supervised reconstruction of the city walls, while Joab saw to the restoration of the buildings. From that time on Jebus was to be known as the holy city of Zion and as the city of David. It was the religious and political capital of the Hebrew kingdom.

The rising fortunes of the Hebrew nation now dictated that its king reign in a degree of splendor. King Hiram of Tyre sent cedar wood and a skilled work force of carpenters and stone masons to build David a palace. Once the palace had been built, however, David became disturbed that the Lord's dwelling among the Israelites was still the relatively obscure and unpretentious ark eight miles from Jerusalem at Kiriath-jearim. The ark, David decided, must be brought to Jerusalem.

The king had messages sent out to all Hebrews, from the border of Egypt to the Pass at Hamath, conveying his intention and inviting them to attend the translation of the ark to the capital. The people were to accompany the ark in a solemn yet joyful procession, escorted by the king's picked troops. The ark was

placed on a new oxen-drawn wagon and two sons of Abinadab
went with it as guards, Ahio walking in front of the vehicle, and
Uzzah alongside it. There were no Levites present. The king and
the royal retinue danced around the ark, singing at the top of their
voices to the accompaniment of lyres, harps, tambourines, castanets, and cymbals.

But then an unfortunate accident occurred. The oxen became
skittish and caused the wagon to tilt. Without thinking, Uzzah put
his hand to the ark to steady it, and at once he was struck down
and died. Even the Levites, whose privilege alone it was to carry
the ark, had never dared touch it; rather, they carried it on their
shoulders by means of shafts.

This misfortune had a profound effect upon David. Fearing
now to take the ark on into Jerusalem, he diverted the procession's
course to the house of the Levite Obed-edom at Gath, twenty-two
miles farther south in the foothills. "The ark may be moved only
by the Levites, since the Lord has chosen them to carry the ark,
and they are always to serve him in his worship" (1 Chr 15:2).

After three months David gathered Israel all together again to
bring the ark up the rest of the way to Jerusalem. This time the
priests and Levites also participated. He summoned the priests
Zadok and Abiathar and the chieftains of the various Levite
clans—Uriel, Asaiah, Joel, Shemiah, Eliel, Aminadab—and
he said:

> You, the heads of the levitical families, must sanctify your-
> selves along with your brethren, and bring the ark of the Lord
> the God of Israel to the place which I have prepared for it.
> Because you were not with us the first time, the wrath of the
> Lord our God burst upon us, for we did not seek him aright. (1
> Chr 15:12–13)

After six paces had been taken, David sacrificed an ox and a
sheep. Like the cantors and the Levite bearers of the ark, David
was wearing a robe of fine linen, and his robe was thrown over the
linen ephod and loincloth of a priest. As the pilgrims' procession
began, with dancing and cries of joy, to return to the city, David
put all his garments aside except for the priestly loincloth. When
they entered Jerusalem, the king and all his retinue were dancing,

leaping, and whirling wildly around the ark, acclaiming God to the sound of trumpets.

When the procession finally reached the tent David had prepared for the ark, Asaph sang a hymn which the king had composed for this occasion. Parts of it live on in three of the psalms and in these lines which follow.

> May the entire earth now sing to the Lord!
> Announce you his salvation day after day;
> Speak of his glory to the other nations;
> Reveal his marvels to every people.
> Let the nations proclaim, "The Lord is king!"
> Let the ocean thunder throughout its vastness,
> Let the fields show delight in all they grow,
> And let the trees in the woods jump for joy;
> For the Lord is to come to judge the world.
> So give praise to the Lord, for he is good,
> And everlasting is his mercy. (1 Chr 16:23–24, 31–34)

Zechariah and eight other Levites accompanied this song on harp and lyre. Asaph clanged the cymbals, and the priests Benaiah and Jahaziel blew the trumpets. At the end of the song holocausts and peace oblations were made. Then David blessed the people in the name of the Lord and distributed to everyone a cut of roast meat, a small piece of bread, and a raisin cake.

Since the ark was now at Gihon on Mount Zion, while the tabernacle was still on the high place at Gibeon, there were temporarily two centers of worship in Israel. At the tabernacle, Zadok and his brother priests conducted the sacrificial rites and offered the morning and evening holocausts. In the background, the musicians Heman and Juduthun would blow the trumpets and clang the cymbals in concert with other musical instruments and with choirs singing hymns. At the ark, David commissioned Asaph and his brothers to conduct a daily, nonsacrificial ritual of praise. Seven priests were appointed to sound the trumpets there, and two men were assigned as keepers of the gate.

Michal, David's first wife, had been gazing out of the palace window watching her husband as he led the ark's procession onto the plateau. As she saw him dancing exuberantly, dressed only in a loincloth, to the sounds of horn, trumpets, cymbals, castanets, harps, and lyres, she felt a strong distaste and waited for an opportunity to scold him for his impropriety.

When he had come into the palace and finished blessing the household, she glanced contemptuously at the loincloth and said, "Today the king of Israel made a spectacle of himself by carrying on like a buffoon and exposing himself in full view of all his maidservants!" (2 Sm 6:20). David rejoined, "It was for the Lord, not for them, that I danced. If my dancing demeaned me in his sight, so be it; but as for the servant girls you have referred to, they will esteem me all the more because of what I did" (2 Sm 6:21–22). For having thus scoffed at her husband's conduct round the ark, Michal remained without child until the day she died.

Aside from this incident, life in David's palace went evenly ahead. The king took other wives and concubines, from whom were born thirteen sons and daughters, Solomon among them.

But David's affection extended beyond those who were his own flesh and blood. He was unable to forget Jonathan and the pact they had made with each other. He inquired whether any of Jonathan's relations had survived and was informed that one of his friend's sons, a cripple named Meribaal, was still alive. David called Meribaal to the court, and ordered that he and his son were to sit at the royal table and take their meals henceforth alongside David's own sons. What was more, the king turned over to Meribaal the properties that belonged to the House of Saul, along with a staff of servants to work the land under the direction of one of Saul's former servants named Ziba. "A kindness for your father Jonathan's sake" (2 Sm 9:7). Overwhelmed by all this favor, the poor man could only voice his astonishment at David's graciousness "to a dead dog like me" (2 Sm 9:8).

David Was Not to Build the Temple

Well settled in his palace now, King David felt that he should collect the materials and the working force which would be required for construction of a great Temple. He said to the prophet Nathan, "I am living in a mansion built of cedar, while the ark of

God's Covenant still stands beneath the awning of a tent of skins"
(2 Sm 7:2). That night, however, God said this to Nathan:

Go and tell my servant David,
It is the Lord himself who asks,
Should it be you who builds me a house?
Ever since I led the Israelites
Out of the land of Egypt till now,
I have never dwelt in any house.
I have lived the life of a wanderer,
My abode a tabernacle or tent.
Yet in all the going about that took place,
Did I ever say to one of the judges
Assigned to look after Israel my people,
Why have you not built me a house of cedar?
Tell David it is the Lord of Hosts
Who now has this to say to him:
I took you from tending the flocks at pasture
To be king of my people Israel.
I have gone with you on your campaigns,
Crushing your enemies before you.
I will give you fame as great as that
Which rivals any other on earth.
And for Israel, my people, I provided a haven
Where, anchors cast, they ride safe from storms.
Invaders shall not any more oppress them,
As was done in the days when I assigned judges
For my people Israel's salvation.
I will give you rest from your adversaries.
The Lord says, I will build you a House,
So that when your days have come to an end
And you fall asleep with your ancestors,
I will still be preserving the seed of your body,
To maintain your sovereignty ever intact.
A Temple to my name will be built by your heir,
And his royal throne I will always protect;
A father to him will I be. And he,
In turn, will be a son to me.

And if he should ever do any evil,
I will punish him as a parent does
In giving a spanking to his child;
But my favor will not be withdrawn from him
As it was from Saul, whom I dethroned.
Your House and your kingdom are going to stand
Safe and secure before me forever.
Your throne has been given you for good. (2 Sm 7:5–16)

When Nathan told David what the Lord had said, the king entered the tent of the ark and prayed: "Who am I and who are the people of my House that you, O Lord, go to such great lengths for me? In your estimation, O Lord, nothing was enough, short of prolonging your servant's House into the far-distant future" (2 Sm 7:18–19).

David's Army

After David had begun to occupy his palace in Jerusalem, his army took the appearance of an invincible force in the Middle East. Joab and Abishai were first and second in command under David, and David himself not seldom took the field in charge of the Hebrew divisions in person. David was not only a supreme strategist, but by the sheer magnetism of his personality he inspired the highest degree of devotion and loyalty in his men.

This had been true ever since the Philistine campaigns in the earliest days of his career. From these days stemmed tales of amazing feats performed by a trio of his followers—tales acquiring a legendary flavor by being celebrated ever afterward.

Such were the anecdotes told: of Hashobeam the Hachmonite, who in one single action put literally hundreds of Philistines out of action by the wielding of his battle-axe; of Eleazar the Ahoite, who after daring the Philistines to advance, stood resolute and alone in a barley field and stoutly stayed the enemy's onrush, saving the day by swinging his sword so fiercely that when the other Israelites returned for the spoils, his numbed fingers were stuck as if frozen to the hilt of his sword; and of Shamma the Hararite, who stationed himself in the middle of a lentil field, and when his fellow soldiers had fallen back and taken flight, with the help of the Lord he turned the battle from defeat into victory.

The army with which David waged his wars and made his conquests was an army of infantrymen who fought with swords and lances and shields, with bows and slings and battle-axes. The army had capable officers and was highly organized into units of hundreds and thousands.

The army's famous elite corps was known as the "Thirty." Like the lions they were among the picked troops, the Thirty turned the tide of battle time after time. During the consolidation of the kingdom they were recruited from the Hebrew tribes alone, but as the empire took shape, membership in the Thirty came to include hero-champions from a variety of ethnic backgrounds. Leaders of the corps of the Thirty were Abishai, Joab's illustrious brother; Amasai, once a spokesman for the Ziklag recruits; and Adina, the commander of the Reubenites. Among others who were honored to serve in this distinguished corps were Asahel, another of Joab's brothers; Benaiah, captain of the king's bodyguard; Naharai, Joab's armor-bearer; and Ishmaiah of Gibeon, a Benjaminite and a kinsman of Saul.

Completing the Conquest of the Promised Land

When the king of Ammon died David courteously sent an embassy to convey his condolences to Hanum, son and heir to the throne. But Hanum had David's envoys arrested as intelligence agents and then released them in a disgraceful condition—half their beards were shaved off and their garments cropped close to their buttocks. David's anger knew no bounds.

Well aware that the king of Israel would take such an insult as a declaration of war, Ammon's new king set out at once to strengthen his country's defensive position and solicit reinforcements. He sent 1,000 talents of silver to Hadadezer, suzerain of Zobah (the part of southern Syria bordering on Phoenicia northward from Damascus), and hired his army and the armies of his vassals. This amounted to 20,000 foot soldiers of the suzerain's plus 13,000 from the vassal states of Maacah and Beth-rehob in upper Transjordania. In addition, there were thousands of chariots.

David was informed of these developments. He chose not to take the field himself, but put Joab and, under him, Abishai, at the head of an army composed both of the regulars and the elite troops of Israel.

The Ammonites drew up in a line a short distance from their capital's gate, while their allies, the Aramaeans of western Syria and the Transjordanians, took up a position out in the open country. Seeing that the battle was to be fought on two fronts, Joab divided the Hebrew force into two units. He ranged the picked troops in front of the allies, while the regulars were to do battle with the Ammonites. If one of the two Hebrew lines were to collapse, the other was to break off its engagement and come to the rescue.

When the battle was joined, Joab's warriors broke through the Aramaean line, killing 22,000 enemy troops. The Ammonites saw their confederates abandoning the field in disarray, and they gave ground before Abishai and the Israelite regulars. Then they drew back through the gate and locked themselves within the city walls. David's army did not then lay siege to the capital, but returned to Jerusalem, there to receive the king's orders and pass the winter.

The Aramaeans regrouped their forces after their defeat. Hadadezer, their suzerain, managed to enlist the backing of other Aramaeans, those of the Euphrates valley in upper Mesopotamia. The combined armies of the Aramaeans were mustered at Helam under the command of Shobach, Hadadezer's general, with as many as 32,000 chariots. At this David called out all of Israel's troops and went with them to engage the enemy at Helam, near the Pass of Hamath. At full strength the Hebrews would have been a striking force of nearly 300,000 men.

In the battle which followed, the array of the Syrians crumbled before the headlong Hebrew onslaught, their ranks dissolving in confusion and disaster. Of their thousands of chariots, 700 were demolished, 1,000 were captured, and untold numbers were put out of commission. Shobach and 40,000 of his troops were left dead on the battlefield, 20,000 of these being foot soldiers, 7,000 being chariot drivers, and the rest probably cavalry. The kingdom of the Aramaean Zobah was crushed, and all his vassals surrendered and sued for peace, becoming subjects or tributaries of David. Damascus was garrisoned.

As prizes of war David took back to Jerusalem the gold shields of Hadadezer's guard, and great quantities of bronze seized in Zobah's towns. All of it was consecrated to the building of the future Temple. Piles of gold, silver, and bronze were also presented to David by Tou, the king of Hamath in the valley of the Orontes River, who was grateful for the destruction of Hadadezer. The dominion of the Israelites now extended north to the Pass of Hamah and east to the Euphrates River.

The war with Ammon was brought to a conclusion in the spring following the battle of Helam. David dispatched Joab with his army and the royal bodyguard to put the Ammonite capital, Rabbah, under siege and lay waste the countryside. He himself remained at Jerusalem. But when Joab's siege had taken the lower city, which contained the town's water supply, the king came down from Jerusalem at the head of the rest of his forces and compelled the capitulation of the capital's acropolis. He found the gold crown of the idol Milcom, an Ammonite god, and took from it a precious stone which he wore on his own head.

The conquest of Ammon seems to have marked the point at which the Hebrew state began its transformation from a kingdom to an empire. From that time on, the reign of David gathered ever-increasing glory. The Aramaeans of the west and east had been crushed and forced to pay tribute. In the Valley of Salt, east of Beer-sheba, Abishai with 18,000 men defeated the Edomites. The Moabites and the Amalekites also were incorporated into David's empire and reduced to tributary status. The Philistines were utterly cowed and their provincial capital of Gath was taken from their hands. Hebrew rule had been established from Egypt to the Euphrates. And to Jerusalem now came the great trophies and rich spoils gathered by the victorious Israelite armies. Stores of iron, bronze, cedar, precious metals, and rare stones were set aside for the building of the Temple. Expert artisans from among the conquered peoples were employed to fashion building materials and Temple furniture, while many unskilled laborers were put to manual work. The labor gangs were made up of Hittites, Amorites, Perizzites, Hivites, and Jebusites who had chosen to live among the Hebrews as proselytes.

Lust and Murder in the Royal Household

During the siege of Rabbah, David had remained in his palace in Jerusalem. One afternoon he rose from his siesta and went for a stroll on the palace roof. From the roof he could see a woman bathing whose great beauty ravished him. David found out that her name was Bathsheba, and that she was the wife of a Hittite mercenary named Uriah, a man distinguished in the king's service. At that moment Uriah was engaged in the hard-fought siege of the Ammonite capital.

The king was aflame with passion. He had Bathsheba brought to him, and he lay with her. Later, when she found out that she had conceived, from her home she sent David the word, "I am with child" (2 Sm 11:5).

David then sent for Uriah. Uriah presented himself at the court, and after some light conversation David suggested that the soldier go home and enjoy the pleasures of domestic life. Uriah departed, and some food from the king's table was sent after him.

But instead of going to his house, the Hittite slept that night on a pallet in the palace portal, where the guardsmen of the king stood duty. David found this out and summoned him, asking why he had passed up this refreshing relief from the ordeal of war. Uriah replied that the ark of the Lord was covered only by a tent, like Israel's troops, and that Joab and his elite were lodged in the open on the field. As a soldier, he surely must not—and he swore he would not—go home to eat and sleep with his wife. The next day David invited Uriah to dinner and made sure to get him drunk. But Uriah slept off his intoxication in the palace portal. Convinced at last that this man would not break his soldier's oath of continence, the king resolved to arrange his death.

David wrote a letter to Joab, stating that Uriah was to be put where the fiercest fighting was likely to occur. The soldiers around him were then to fall back, leaving him to be struck down and killed. Joab accordingly detailed the brave mercenary to a post where the most formidable of the city's defenders were known to be. When these defenders sallied forth, Uriah, abandoned by his comrades, was overwhelmed and killed. At the news of her husband's death, Bathsheba went into mourning. When the period of mourning was over, David had her brought to the palace, where she bore him a son.

The Lord was displeased with David and sent the prophet Nathan to give the king his judgment. Nathan presented to him the case of a man so poor that he had nothing to his name but a lamb, raised in his house for the delight of him and his children. This pet was taken away from him by a very wealthy man who butchered it to be served as a delicacy to a guest in his mansion. David was extremely angry to hear of such a thing done in his kingdom. He roared, "That man deserves to die for his want of compassion, and let there be fourfold restitution made for the lamb!" (2 Sm 12:5–6). Then Nathan bluntly broke out with the truth:

> You are that man! And now the Lord has had this to say: "I anointed you king and gave you the wealth of a kingdom; but you have played the knave with Uriah the Hittite by taking his wife from him and having him struck down by Ammonite blades. So now the sword will ever hang over you and your House. What you did in secret I will do in full view of all Israel and in the full light of the sun." (2 Sm 12:7–10, 12)

Humbled and repentant, David confessed his sin. Nathan said that the Lord was not going to strike him dead, but that the child of his adultery must die.

The baby fell gravely ill, and David pleaded for the infant with the Lord. He entered upon a total fast, and slept on sacking spread on the bare ground. Although the officials of his court gathered round him, he would not heed their pleas to rise and eat with them. Then, seven days after birth, the baby died.

Resigned to the loss of his son, David bathed and anointed himself, put on fresh clothing, and went into the sanctuary where he prostrated himself before the Lord. He returned to the palace, ate, and consoled Bathsheba. In time she conceived again and gave birth to Solomon, whom the Lord named Jedidiah, the "beloved of Yahweh."

And now, perhaps as part of the evils the Lord had said would be stirred up within his House to punish him, David was to be tortured by a display of lust in his eldest son, Amnon, and by an act of fratricide committed by his third son, Absalom.

Absalom had a strikingly beautiful virgin sister whose name was Tamar. The two were David's children by his wife Maacah, a princess in her own right since she was the daughter of Tamai, sovereign of Geshur, the land east of the Sea of Galilee (modern Golan Heights).

Amnon conceived a passionate love for his half-sister Tamar, and yearned to have intercourse with her. Following the suggestion of his cousin Jonadab, he feigned illness. When the king inquired after his health Amnon requested that Tamar be assigned to prepare his food, saying that in this way perhaps his sluggish appetite would be restored.

So David told Tamar to go to the apartment where Amnon lay abed pretending to be ill. She kneaded dough and made cakes, but when she served him he claimed he could not eat in the presence of others. Everyone except Tamar left his quarters, and she served the meal to him in the inner room where he had his bed. Suddenly, while she was handing him the plate, he seized her and drew her down with him. She cried out for him not to violate her virginity, an act which would both shame her and ostracize him from decent Hebrew society. But Amnon was deaf to her pleading. He brutally overpowered and raped her.

Immediately afterward he experienced a revulsion toward her, and his prior infatuation was turned into a feeling of bitter hatred. Brusquely he ordered her to leave him, but she refused, protesting that such a dismissal would be an even greater wrong than that which he had already done her. At that, he bawled out to the orderly stationed outside the door of his quarters, "Get rid of this woman for me; put her out and bar the door after her!" (2 Sm 13:17).

Poor Tamar went weeping and wailing to Absalom's house, her long-sleeved gown torn and tattered and her hands thrown up to cover and hide her head. The king was angry when he learned of

Amnon's despicable conduct, but he refused to chastise his beloved firstborn. Absalom, however, would not even speak to Amnon. He hated his brother for what he had done and calmly awaited an opportunity to avenge the crime.

Two years later Absalom's opportunity arrived. The occasion was Absalom's annual sheep-shearing ceremony at Baal-hazor near Ephraim. It was to be a festive event to which the king and his courtiers would be invited. Absalom knew that his father would decline to attend so as not to be a burden upon his son's hospitality; but he secured the king's consent for Amnon and his other brothers to attend.

The banquet was held, and when Amnon had drunk a good deal of wine, Absalom had his men kill him. The other princes leaped on their mules and dashed away. At first the king received the garbled news that Absalom had slain all his brothers, but later the true report came in that only Amnon was dead, and that Absalom was taking refuge at the court of his mother's father, the ruler of Geshur. Absalom remained in exile for three years, during which time David mourned for his firstborn and refused to be consoled.

When Joab at last noticed a change of heart taking place in the king, he resorted to a ruse. He sent a woman dressed in mourning garments before David to plead for the pardon of a son who had wantonly taken his brother's life. David gave her his promise that the protective mantle of the king's mercy would be thrown over the culprit. At that, the woman suggested that by the same token Absalom ought to be released from exile. David asked her, "Was it Joab who put you up to this?" (2 Sm 14:19). And she confessed that it was. So the king summoned Joab and told him to get Absalom and bring him home. But that was as far as the king would go in amnesty: The prince would have the freedom of the capital and the kingdom, but he would not be welcome at the palace nor received at court. In a word, his banishment was lifted, but he had not regained the favor of the king.

The Revolt of Absalom

Absalom lived in Jerusalem for two years without being allowed to come into his father's presence. When the second year had passed he sent for Joab to intercede for his restoration to David's good graces, but Joab refused to come. Desperate for attention, the disgruntled prince had his men set fire to one of Joab's barley fields. Absalom then told the angered Joab that his state of mind and heart had become unbearable—it would have been far better for him to have remained in distant Geshur than live shamed in Jerusalem; it would even have been better to have been judged guilty by his father and put to the sword. Joab reported the prince's thoughts and feelings to the king. At this, David called his son before him and forgave him.

But Absalom began to toy with the idea of one day sitting on David's throne and ruling the kingdom in his stead. So he embarked upon a course of intrigue calculated to provide him with power to shake the throne and himself grasp the reins of government. The foundation on which he built his hope was an accident of Palestinian history and geography: the fact that the northern Hebrew tribes had developed hostility toward the southern tribes. King Saul, a man of the tribe of Benjamin, had been the northern tribes' champion—liberator of Jabesh-gilead, victor at Michmash, fallen on the battlefield at Gilboa. King David hailed from the southernmost tribe of Judah, and the northern tribes resented the preeminence that had come to Judah on account of David. Absalom labored to widen the rift in the nation by stirring up the northerners to greater feelings of discontent and resentment. He wanted to see Israel actually pit itself against Judah. Through Absalom's exploitation of this antagonism, the ghost of Saul, as it were, had come to flog David with a cat-o-nine-tails.

Absalom began by drawing attention to himself. Whereas the king's sons normally rode mounted on mules, Absalom went about in a stallion-drawn chariot preceded by a retinue of fifty runners. He made a point of frequenting the roadway leading up to the palace and speaking to the northerners who came to present grievances or lodge lawsuits. He always bestowed a kiss and a handclasp on those who approached to pay him their respects. He spoke against the king, saying that corruption was rife among the king's deputies, and often he would sigh, "Ah, if only it were given me to administer justice in the realm!" (2 Sm 15:4). He spent four years thus cultivating the friendship of the northern tribes and undermining their loyalty to David's throne. Then, finally, he considered the situation ripe for him to strike a blow.

He told his father that he had made a vow to offer sacrifice at Hebron, and begged his leave to go there for that purpose. David gave him leave. Two hundred of Absalom's followers went with him from Jerusalem, not knowing what he was up to, but they were not left long in doubt. While Absalom was offering his sacrifices, he was sending couriers to all of Israel's tribes with the message that when the trumpet sounded at Hebron, he would be declared king. Quickly the conspiracy against the throne gathered strength, not only in numbers but personages. Even Ahitophel, David's own counselor, came to Hebron and joined the faction.

David Flees from Jerusalem

As soon as David became aware that the whole of Israel had defected to his son, he made preparations to evacuate Jerusalem. He had hoped to spare the capital from probable assault and massacre. "If we depart quickly, before he mounts an attack, the city will not be put to the sword" (2 Sm 15:14). David, then about sixty years of age, went forth on foot from his palace, leaving behind him only his ten concubines. At the edge of the city his entourage gathered round him: Benaiah's Cherethites and Pelethites, his bodyguard, and a knot of loyal officials and devoted people. Some of his mercenaries, 600 strong, under command of Ittai the Gittite, also marched out to him. David said to Ittai, "You are a foreigner, an exile who has but recently entered my service. Go back, and take your fellow countrymen with you. The Lord bless you for your kindness and fidelity" (2 Sm 15:19-20). David even said that Ittai was free to give allegiance to the usurper if he desired. But the captain of the mercenaries swore that he and his men would remain loyal to David whether they lived or died.

Zadok the priest and the Levites were also present with David. They had the ark with them, which they set down beside the priest Abiathar. But the king bade them take up the ark and go back into the city with it. "Should I find favor in the eyes of the Lord, he will let me return to see it and the tabernacle again" (2 Sm 15:25).

David's intention was to stay in the barrens until Zadok and Abiathar sent him word about the situation in the city.

The king's party crossed the Kidron Valley. While they were making their way up the Mount of Olives—all of them in tears, and David with his feet bare and his head shrouded—a messenger arrived with the news that Ahitophel, the king's trusted adviser, was taking part in Absalom's rebellion. When they reached the summit of the hill a friend of David, Hushai the Archite, hurried up from the city to meet them with his tunic torn and earth strewn on his head. He wanted to go with David into exile, but David told him to go back to Jerusalem and blunt the counsels of Ahitophel. He should welcome Absalom and offer him his services. Then he would be able to play the part of an informer, gathering information to be sent to David through the sons of the two priests, Zadok and Abiathar. Hushai agreed and got back to Jerusalem just as Absalom and his men were entering the city.

When the king and his supporters had travelled a little beyond the summit of the Mount of Olives, Ziba, the steward of Meribaal, arrived with supplies—a pair of saddled asses laden with 200 loaves of bread, 100 cakes of raisins, some fruit, and a skin of wine. He said that the asses were for the use of the king's family, the bread and the fruit for the soldiers to eat, and the skin of wine for people to drink who might otherwise collapse in the passage through the wilderness. He added that his master, Meribaal, had decided to remain in Jerusalem in the hopes that the kingdom would now be restored to him, as Saul's grandson. When David heard this he angrily transferred ownership of all the holdings of Meribaal to Ziba.

Farther on along the Bahurim road leading down to Jericho, a Benjaminite named Shimei came up to the king's procession and rained down curses on them as they were wending their way through the valley. Shimei kept spewing out venom at David, even though the king was surrounded by his soldiers, shouting, "Away, away, you man of blood and infamy! God is paying you back for spilling the blood of the House of Saul; for the throne you usurped has now passed to Absalom" (2 Sm 16:7–8). Nettled by these insults, Abishai wanted to run up the hillside and lop off Shimei's head. But David said, "No, let him curse me if that be

God's will. If my son now seeks my life, how can those curses do me harm? Who knows, the Lord may yet repay me with good for having been maligned this day" (2 Sm 16:11–12). Shimei kept pace with their progress down the mountain, all the while shrieking maledictions, flinging stones, and scattering dirt upon them. At length, however, the royal retinue arrived at a place where the king and all with him could rest and be refreshed.

Meanwhile, Absalom had taken over David's palace in Jerusalem. Hushai the Archite met him there and hailed him with an enthusiastic "Long live the king! Long live the king!" (2 Sm 16:16). Absalom asked him why he had not left the city with his friend, David, and Hushai replied that he felt his place was with him whom the Lord and Israel had chosen. As he had served David, so would he serve David's son. He was invited to join the council of elders, where he shared preeminence with Ahitophel.

In the council Ahitophel took the lead and advised two courses of action. He thought that it would be wise, first of all, for Absalom to do something dramatic to make clear to Israel his antagonism to his father. Thus he would secure to himself the absolute and irrevocable support of all the people. Ahitophel suggested that a suitable step would be to lie with his father's concubines. Accordingly, a tent was pitched on the palace roof where the whole city could see Absalom going to lie with David's women.

Ahitophel also advised Absalom to give him 12,000 troops and send them off in pursuit of the deposed king. David was likely to be fatigued and discouraged, and therefore could be taken easily. David alone had to be killed; those with him could be left unscathed and brought back to Absalom like a bride returning to her husband.

These proposals appealed to the council; but Absalom, wanting to be certain of following the most judicious course, called upon Hushai to give his opinion. Hushai disagreed with Ahitophel on the second point. He said to Absalom:

> You know that your father and his men are champions in the practice of the military art, and they will be fierce as a bear defending her cubs. David will not have rested his army at nightfall; right now he has taken cover and set an ambush.

Should our army sustain losses at the very outset, we are sure to be defeated. It would be better by far for your majesty to go in person to lead not just a small force, but all of Israel's fighting strength. You will then come upon him like the dew that falls upon the grass, leaving him no escape. If David should seek refuge in a town, we will put ropes to both walls and buildings and drag them down in pieces to the wadi. (2 Sm 17:8–9, 11–13)

Absalom and his council accepted Hushai's advice. The crestfallen Ahitophel, feeling disgraced and despondent, rode off to his home town and committed suicide. And as the Lord intended, Absalom set himself upon the course that would lead to his doom.

Hushai informed the priests Zadok and Abiathar of the discussion and decision of the council and asked them to warn David. "Do not camp tonight either on the plains or in the wilderness, but get across the Jordan as quickly as possible. If you do not do this, king and army will be destroyed" (2 Sm 17:16). The runners who carried this message from the priests to David were seen by one of Absalom's men, and Absalom sent some of his servants to go and catch them. They managed to elude pursuit, however, and the message was delivered.

David and his followers reached the far side of the Jordan before daylight and headed onward toward Mahanaim. There three men—one from Rabbah, another from Lodebar, the third from Gilead—greeted David with provisions and supplies: wheat and barley; roasted grain and meat; beans and lentils; honey, butter, and cheese; sheep and oxen; couches, coverlets, and earthenware. David was safely headquartered at Mahanaim by the time Absalom's forces were fording the Jordan, thirty-five miles away.

The Inglorious Death of Absalom

King David reviewed his troops in preparation for the upcoming battle. He appointed leaders and then broke down the army into three divisions under the command of Joab, Abishai, and Ittai the Gittite. In the hearing of all, David ordered the three commanders to spare Absalom's life. The soldiers told the king that he must not go into battle with them, for the enemy would stop at nothing to kill him. "You are worth ten thousand of us. Better that you stay garrisoned with our reserves in the town" (2 Sm 18:3). David consented to their wishes, and took up a position at the double gate as his troops moved out.

The battle was fought in a forest near Mahanaim. The army of Absalom, commanded by Absalom's cousin Amasa, met disaster there, losing 20,000 men. Evidently, more of them perished while fleeing in the tangled undergrowth of the forest than fell victim to the sword. In the confusion, Absalom, mounted on his mule, lost contact with his bodyguard and encountered a squad of David's men. As he was racing away from them his hair got snarled in the dense, low-hanging limbs of a huge oak. His mule passed from under him and galloped off, leaving him dangling in the air by the hair of his head.

One of the soldiers told Joab of Absalom's plight. Joab asked the soldier why he had not cut Absalom down to the ground and killed him, but the soldier stated flatly that he would not have dared to slay the king's son no matter what the reward. Brushing aside the soldier's scruple, Joab seized three lances and went and thrust them into Absalom's heart. He then had his armor-bearers cut the usurper down and finish him off. They cast the corpse into a deep pit and heaped up a huge cairn over the grave. Finally Joab had a trumpet blast sounded to end the pursuit of Absalom's men.

Ahimaaz son of Zadok the priest wanted to run to Mahanaim to break the news of the successful outcome of the battle to the king. But Joab cautioned him that the king would not receive this as good news, "for the king's son is dead" (2 Sm 18:20). He turned to a Cushite soldier and ordered him to "go and tell the king what you have seen" (2 Sm 18:21). When the Cushite started running, Ahimaaz started too and soon passed him.

David was sitting by the town gate when the lookout on the tower caught sight of the two running figures. Ahimaaz arrived first and announced the victory, but when David asked, "Is the youth Absalom all right?" (2 Sm 18:29). Ahimaaz side-stepped the question. "There was a great uproar when your servant Joab sent me off, but I don't know what it was about" (2 Sm 18:29). Then the Cushite came up and he, too, reported the happy outcome of the battle. When the king again asked, "Is all well with young Absalom?" (2 Sm 18:32) the Cushite messenger blurted out the truth. "May all my lord the king's adversaries and all who ever dare rise against him share the fate of that young man!" (2 Sm 18:32).

At this, David shuddered and made his way up to the tower. He burst into tears and groaned "O my son Absalom! Absalom my son! Would that I had died in your place, my son Absalom! O Absalom my son!" (2 Sm 19:1). Word reached Joab and the army that the king was grieving for his son. So despite the glorious victory that had been gained, the day turned into one of sadness—the army stole into the town as if they had been shamefully defeated.

Joab could not endure this show of tenderness for a usurper who had merely received his just reward. He climbed to the tower to confront the king, who with his head shrouded was sitting there wailing, "My son Absalom! Absalom my son! O my son!" (2 Sm 19:5). Joab said to him:

> You are making your troops ashamed of this day on which they have saved your life and the lives of your sons, daughters, wives, and concubines. They are sad because of your love for those who hate you and your hatred for those who love you. You are making it plain today that your officers and soldiers mean nothing to you; were Absalom alive and all of us lying dead on the field, you would surely be pleased. Come on, get up, and go out to reassure your troops. If you fail to go, there will not be a single man remaining with you tonight. And this would be the worst misfortune that ever happened to you. (2 Sm 19:6–8)

Then the king stood up and went down to take his seat at the gate, where the whole army assembled before him.

David Returns to Jerusalem

When the Israelite soldiers who had survived defeat in the forest near Mahanaim went home, a good deal of wrangling took place among their tribes. The sentiment of the people swung round to calling David back as their sovereign lord. The king asked the priests Zadok and Abiathar to ask the elders of Judah to invite him to return. Then David himself invited Amasa, the commander of Absalom's army, to come and serve in place of Joab as commander of the royal army.

A series of dramatic incidents took place at the Jordan ford on David's way back to Jerusalem. The men of Judah had assembled at Gilgal and 1,000 Benjaminites were gathered at the ford to meet him. Among the latter was Shimei, who had previously cursed David and thrown stones at him along the Bahurim road. He begged the king to forgive him. Abishai still thought that Shimei deserved death for his conduct, but David spared the life of the Benjaminite, saying, "On a day such as this, should anyone in Israel be put to death? Today I know for certain that I am indeed Israel's king" (2 Sm 19:23).

Also present among the Benjaminites was Ziba, the steward of Saul. The fifteen sons and twenty servants of Ziba manfully engaged themselves in ferrying the king's family across the Jordan as well as performing many other tasks.

Upon this scene now came Meribaal, who had neither washed his clothes nor cared for his physical appearance since David's flight from the palace. He protested that he had been slandered by his servant Ziba. He had, in fact, intended to join the royal exodus from Jerusalem, but Ziba had left him behind. David now ruled that Ziba should share the properties of Saul's family with his master. But Meribaal said, "Let him take it all, as long as the king has come home safely!" (2 Sm 19:31).

Barzillai the Gileadite had also come down to meet David at the ford. The king begged his old friend, who had brought him provisions when he was fleeing to Mahanaim, to come up to Jerusalem and stay there with him. But Barzillai excused himself, saying that he did not have long to live, that his senses were failing, that his appetite was poor, and that he was hard of hearing. He would be a burden. All he wanted was to see the king safely across the Jordan and then return to his home to die near the graves of his parents. He had a son, however, who would go up to Jerusalem in his stead and remain there in the king's service. David kissed and blessed Barzillai before he went his way from the ford.

By now, half the people of Israel had joined the men of Judah at Gilgal, and a quarrel broke out between the two rival factions. Judah maintained that the king was their relative, and Israel contended that their tribes not only had a vested interest in the king but were Judah's seniors. Israel also claimed that they had also been first to speak of bringing him back.

Just then in the highlands of Ephraim a Benjaminite wretch named Sheba trumpeted the start of another rebellion against David. The men of Israel disappeared from the king's side and went to join Sheba, while the men of Judah stayed to escort David to the capital.

Once he had returned to his palace, David separated his ten violated concubines and kept them under guard. Though he continued to provide for them, he never went in to them again.

Something had to be done immediately, however, about the seditionist Sheba. The king summoned his newly appointed commander, Amasa, and directed him to gather the troops of Judah within three days. Amasa failed to do this, and David, concerned about the danger at hand, ordered Abishai to take the elite guard and hunt the insurrectionist Sheba down. They set out—the Cherethites and Pelethites and some of David's other warriors, including Joab.

On their march Joab happened to meet up with Amasa, whom he killed through trickery: Joab turned toward Amasa as if to greet him in a brotherly fashion, and then, taking hold of Amasa's beard as if to give him a kiss, he plunged his sword into Amasa's belly. There was no need to strike a second time—Amasa died instantly in a great pool of his blood.

Neither Joab nor his brother Abishai so much as paused; they hurried on in pursuit of Sheba. The troops coming up behind them, however, were stopping to look at Amasa's butchered body where it lay in the middle of the road. One of Joab's troopers shouted, "Forward, all who are for Joab, and for David!" (2 Sm 20:11) and dragged the bloody remains of Amasa off the road and into a field where he covered them with a cloak. Not a single dissenting voice was raised. The soldiers all followed after Joab, who thus by his violent deed again attained command of David's army, and in spite of the king regained his former status.

Sheba fled frantically up through the Hebrew kingdom to its northern limit, where, close to Dan, he was brought to bay in the town of Abel. The town was besieged, and rather than lose their lives the inhabitants of Abel cut off the head of Sheba and tossed it down from the rampart. In that way the rebellion of Israel came to an end.

Visitations that Occurred in David's Reign

Several visitations, or manifestations of the Lord's wrath, befell the people during David's long reign. The first of these was a three-year famine. David besought the Lord for the reason why the famine was taking place, and the Lord revealed, "There is blood on Saul and his family for putting the Gibeonites to death" (2 Sm 21:1). Saul had unsuccessfully tried to wipe them out. In so doing he had violated the solemn oath sworn by Joshua in the name of the Israelites that they would live in peace forever with the Gibeonites. The Gibeonite survivors had cursed the Hebrews for their infidelity.

David summoned the remnant of the oppressed Gibeonite people and asked them what could be done to make amends. They replied that they would take neither gold nor silver as reparation; they demanded that vengeance be exacted on Saul's family. They told David to designate seven of Saul's sons for execution.

For Jonathan's sake the king spared Meribaal, Saul's grandson. He singled out two sons of Saul by Saul's concubine Rizpah and five of Saul's grandsons by his daughter Merab. At the start of the barley harvest the Gibeonites took these seven and impaled them "on the mountain of God" (2 Sm 21:9), near the tabernacle. Rizpah, distraught and dressed in sackcloth, laid a shroud over the site of their deaths. She frightened away the scavenger birds and beasts that gathered, and kept vigil there until the rains came which signaled the end of the famine. When told what Rizpah had done, David had the bones of Saul and Jonathan conveyed from Jabesh-gilead and put them with the remains of the seven sons killed at Gibeon. He then had them all buried together in the tomb of Kish, Saul's father.

The second visitation was a disaster that came upon the nation because David had called for a census. The reason why the king's action was sinful is not entirely clear. It is possible that the census-taking was an expression of a lack of faith on David's part that God would really fulfill his ancient promise to make Israel as numerous as the stars in the heavens and the sands of the seashore.

Joab objected to David's plan to take the census and demanded, "Why should this guilt be brought on Israel?" (1 Chr 21:3). But David overruled him. So Joab took his senior officers and went off to register the size of the Hebrew population. He began with Transjordania from the Arnon in the south to Kadesh on the Orontes in the far north, and then passed down through Canaan proper all the way from Dan to Beersheba, that is, from the region near Tyre and Sidon down to and through the Negeb.

The figures given for this census vary from 1,100,000 to 800,000 for Israel, and from 500,000 to 370,000 for Judah. The larger figure for Israel is presented in 1 Chronicles and the larger figure for Judah in 2 Samuel. The census took account only of adult males, that is, men who were twenty years of age or older and able to draw a sword, and no enumeration of the Benjaminites or the Levites was made. Therefore, the total population, including women, children, and younger and older men, could well have been three or four times greater.

David went before the Lord and admitted having committed a grave sin. "Forgive your servant this fault; I have been very fool-ish" (2 Sm 24:10). Through the prophet Gad he was given his choice of one of three punishments: three years of famine, three months of flight before an enemy, or three days of pestilence. David chose the three days of pestilence, preferring, he said, to fall into the hands of a merciful God rather than into the hands of men.

The punishment came at the time of the wheat harvest. A plague arose in the country which killed 70,000 Hebrews within the space of three days. Though David had asked that vengeance for his sin fall on him and his family alone, rather than on the people, the Lord spared Jerusalem out of love for the holy city.

The prophet Gad came again to David and announced that the
Lord wished an altar built on the threshing-floor of Araunah on
the top of Mount Moriah.

The Jebusite Araunah was threshing wheat when he saw the
king coming up to him with his council. He bowed low to the
ground, and David told him that he wanted to buy the threshing
floor and build an altar of sacrifice upon it to stay the course of
the plague. Araunah at once acceded to the king's request. "Pay
me whatever you think is right. I will also give you my team of
oxen for the sacrifice along with their wooden yoke and threshing
sledge for the building of a fire" (2 Sm 24:22). The king made it
plain he was not asking for any donation. "I have to pay you the
fair price in money and in full, as it will not do for me to make
an offering to my God that costs me nothing" (2 Sm 24:24). David
paid Aranauh 600 shekels of gold for the site, plus fifty shekels of
silver for the oxen and equipment.

When the altar had been built and holocausts and peace sacrifices set there, fire came down upon them from heaven. The angel
of God's anger then sheathed his sword, and the Lord stilled the
plague throughout the country.

At this time, the tabernacle and the holocaust altar were still on
the high place of Gibeon. Fearing God's anger, David had not
dared to go there during the three-day plague. But now that he
had acquired the threshing-floor of Araunah and an altar had been
built there, the king made a momentous decision—the ark, the
tabernacle, and the holocaust altar would all be brought together
at this place, which would be the site of the future Temple of God.
"Here shall be the house of the Lord and here the altar of holocaust
for Israel" (1 Chr 21:30).

The Levites and the Temple

The tribe of Levi had three main clans, stemming from Gershon,
Kohath, and Merari, Levi's three sons. The clan with the highest
religious and historical destiny was that of Kohath, for from Kohath's son Amram had come Moses and Aaron. The sons of Aaron
through Eleazar and Ithamar were the high priests of Israel. Zadok,

David's priest, was of the line of Eleazar, and it would be his descendant Azariah who would one day serve as Solomon's priest in the Temple.

The priests were to preside over the sanctuary and observe the ancient ritual of the tent of meeting, consecrating the holy things, performing the ritual atonement, burning incense they themselves had prepared from a mixture of spices, and offering the holocausts.

But all the Levites were to have roles to play in the new Temple. Of the 38,000 Levites thirty years of age or older who were alive at this time (excluding the priests), 24,000 were assigned as cantors to conduct the ritual services, 4,000 to playing the Lord's praises on instruments that David designed, 4,000 to being keepers of the Temple gates, and 6,000 to acting as scribes or judges.

These Levites were to have other duties as well. They were to be at the disposal of the priests in the courts and chambers, taking turns assisting them with the purifications, the rows of show-bread, the fine wheaten flour, and the unleavened cakes of flour and oil.

All the Levites—both priests and helpers—were to take turns glorifying the Lord in the divine services held each morning and evening, and on the sabbath. They were also to superintend the holocausts at the new moon festival and the solemn feasts of Weeks and Tabernacles.

Asaph the Gershonite, Heman the Kohathite, and Jeduthun the Korahite were appointed as the leaders of the cantors. They composed hymns of praise, and sang and prophesied to the sound of harp, lyre, and cymbal. Asaph, Heman, and Jeduthun trained their kinsmen—twenty-four bands of twelve Levites each—to sing the praise of God in the Temple service. Their compositions, whether original or sung to an already well-known melody, were scored for lyres, harps, flutes, oboes, trumpets, and percussion instruments, with the octave lyre giving the beat. Robed in fine linen, the cantors were to sit to the east of the altar and there, under the direction of the choirmasters, send up praise, penitence, and thanksgiving to the Lord. The cantors would be subject to duty night and day, and therefore would live in Jerusalem.

The gatekeepers were closely associated with the cantors and their choirs. They were to be the guardians of the place of worship and act as ushers and watchmen whenever the people would gather for ritual services. They were to stand guard at the sanctuary's four thresholds—east, west, north, and south—according to their shifts of duty. At dark they would close the holy place and at dawn open it again.

Some of them would take care of the Temple furniture; some were to look after the sacred supplies of flour, wine, oil, incense, and spices; still others were charged with tending the baked goods, in particular the loaves of offering that were to be set out fresh in rows every sabbath. The Gershomites, descendants of Moses, were assigned to keep watch over the storehouse of consecrated treasure that had been donated to the Temple by Samuel, Abner, David, the tribal chieftains, the army officers, and Joab.

David and the Psalter

David continued to compose songs to be sung before the ark. These songs were eventually collected in the Psalter, a book containing 150 psalms from a variety of sources, with musical notations and rubrical directions for their use in Temple worship. The Psalter was the Temple hymnbook. The psalms differ in length and literary form, and most often express praise, supplication, and thanksgiving. Sometimes they may also express lamentation, wisdom teaching, and prophecy.

As we saw earlier, when David was bringing the ark up to Zion, David had written a hymn of praise and given it to Asaph and his kin to sing. Parts of this song were later incorporated into Psalms 96, 105, and 106. How many other songs in the Psalter are from the quill of the poet-king is not certain. Tradition has attributed seventy-three of the 150 psalms to David because the inscriptions of these psalms bear his name. But this may only mean that they were dedicated in his honor. The following song, however, which is very much the same as Psalm 18, is explicitly ascribed to David in 2 Samuel:

The Lord is my rock, my oaken bulwark.
I place all my trust in the strength of my God—

A bonelike sheath, a horn of defense,
Raising me 'high to where I am safe.
O my savior, you keep me from the violence of sin
And then, when I turn to you in praise,
I am protected from my foes.
When overcome by some deadly hazard—
Plunged in a ghastly, careening maelstrom
And suffocating in death's strangling coils—
If in my distress I cry out to the Lord,
Calling out to my God with all my strength,
My voice and my cry will be heard in his Temple.
When the earth lies in throes of quivering and quaking
And the underpinnings of the mountains are shaken,
They are trembling at the sight of his angry face,
Of his nostrils blowing out billows of smoke,
And his mouth spewing bursts of devouring flames
That fiercely burn all there is to embers.
The Lord rouses himself, he is coming down,
A black mist swirling beneath his feet.
He is borne along by the cherubim,
And goes forth gliding on the wings of the wind,
Hidden from sight by the sheltering pall
Of a rack of gathering clouds in the sky.
Wherever he looms up there are lightning flashes
And the land all about is charred to ashes.
The Lord hurls thunderclaps down from the sky,
Thus making his voice heard from above.
He is gathering arrows and will let them fly
To scatter those who dare look upon him.
He pursues them with his lightning flashes.
The ocean's waters flood over the land,
Leaving the beds of the deep swept bare.
The foundations of the world are left exposed
In the wake of the commotion caused by the Lord,
By the blast of the wind of his angry breath.
Yet he reaches from on high and takes hold of me
To draw me out of the roaring waters.
He saves me from enemies too strong for me.

He comes to my help when disaster threatens,
Making himself a mainstay for me.
He leads me forth, where I am free;
And he does all this because I please him.
The Lord rewards me for doing what is right,
Repays me for having kept my hands clean,
For having stayed on the paths of the Lord,
And not reeked of impiety in the presence of God.
I have kept his decrees before my eyes,
My appearance is blameless as he looks upon me.
He will keep my iniquity far from me
And give me back as I have given—
Such cleanness as he shall see in my hands.
If I am holy, you are holy with me;
If I am sinless, you lay no blame.
But you discomfit him who does wrong.
People who are humble you are willing to save,
But the arrogant you will humiliate.
O Lord, you are the lamp by which I see:
You illumine the dark recesses of my life.
By your light I am readied to make my charge;
I leap over the wall with the help of God.
Yes, he is our God—his way is perfect;
When tried in the fire, his word shows no dross.
He is a shield for those who hope in him.
Who else is the rock but him, our God?
He alone is almighty who is our God—
The God who has armed and equipped me with strength
And smoothed out the blameless path I have followed.
He makes my feet like the swift-running stag's,
To hold me poised on the highland heights.
He trains my hands for the weapons of battle,
And makes my arms like a strong bronze bow.
For my safety you have girded me with a buckler.
Your constant care increases my power:
The steps I take are longer now,
And my ankles are stronger, as suits my new pace.
I chase my enemies, wearing them out

And not turning back till they are destroyed.
I strike them down till they rise no more,
Till they lie beneath my feet where they fell.
You have girded me with the strength I need to wage war.
You have made my opponents cringe before me,
And made my foes show their backs to me,
So that thus I could wipe out my foes.
Though they clamor to be rescued, there is none to heed them;
Though they cry to the Lord, there is no reply.
I will grind them as fine as dust in the square;
I will trample upon them like mud in the streets.
You will relieve me of strife in my people,
And see that I am placed at the head of nations.
Foreign peoples will be subjected to me;
In vain will they have offered resistance.
The non-Hebrews will show themselves faint-hearted
And huddle together in hiding places.
Life to the Lord! Blessed be my rock!
You let me have my vengeance, O God.
You subjected nations to my rule.
You allowed me to baffle my enemies,
And raised me high above my opponents.
You delivered me from men's viciousness.
So to you, O Lord, I give thanks forever,
And I sing a canticle to your name,
Celebrating how often the king has been saved,
And your love displayed toward the one you anointed,
Toward David and toward his heirs forever. (2 Sm 22:2–51)

Since the Temple worship was cast into form under David's personal direction, the Psalter can certainly be presumed to have taken shape, at least to some extent, as the work of his hands. David described himself as "a singer of the songs of Israel" (2 Sm 23:1), and is known to have possessed considerable musical talent. His life formed the subject matter of many of the psalms, especially those with Davidic inscriptions. There are many instances of this: Psalm 3 deals with his escape from Absalom; Psalm 7, with Benjaminite enmity toward him; Psalm 8, with divine deliverance

from his enemies and from Saul in particular; Psalm 34, with the
madness he feigned in order to throw a Philistine ruler off guard;
Psalm 51, with the rebuke given him by Nathan for having committed adultery with Bathsheba; Psalm 52, with his betrayal to
Saul by Doeg the Edomite; Psalm 54, with the offer of the Ziphites
to turn him over to Saul; Psalm 56, with his detention by the
Philistines in Gath; Psalm 57, with his escape from Saul in the
cave; Psalm 58, with Saul's sending of agents to kill him in his own
house; Psalm 60, with the war with Zobah and the Aramaeans;
Psalm 63, with the life he led in the barrens of Judah; and Psalm
142, with the time he spent in the cave hiding from Saul.

David's Latter Years

King David was becoming quite old. He was unable to keep
warm, no matter how many blankets he was covered with. His
servants thought to solve this problem by finding him a beautiful
young wife who would warm him by the heat of her body upon
his breast. After searching throughout the tribes of Israel, on the
Plain of Jezreel they found Abishag of Shunem, a woman of sur-
passing beauty. Abishag married David and took care of him,
looking after all his needs.

Adonijah, the fourth of David's sons born at Hebron, was am-
bitious for his father's throne. Just as Absalom had done, Adonijah
took to driving a chariot team with fifty men running in front of
him. Adonijah even made secret plans with Abiathar the priest
and Joab to seize the kingdom. But he failed to win the support
of the priest Zadok, the prophet Nathan, Shimei's Benjaminites,
the champions of the Thirty, and Benaiah, the commander of the
guard.

Adonijah arranged a sacrificial feast near the Fuller's Spring. He
invited all his brothers except Solomon. He also invited all the men
of Judah in the king's service except Nathan and Benaiah. Nathan
took advantage of this situation and went in alarm to Bathsheba,
Solomon's mother.

Have you not heard? Haggith's son Adonijah is making himself
king. If you want to save your life and your son Solomon's life,

go right to King David and demand of him, "Did you not give me your promise on oath that your son Solomon would become king after you, that he would be the one to sit on your throne? Why then, is Adonijah holding a feast without your knowledge at which he is arrogating to himself the role of king?" (1 Kgs 1:11–19)

Bathsheba rushed to the king's chamber and lodged her protest, concluding it with these words:

All Israel is waiting for you to make known who it is who will sit on the throne after your royal majesty. If you do not reveal your decision now, I and my son Solomon will be considered criminals when my lord the king goes to sleep with his fathers. (1 Kgs 1:20–21)

Nathan, following her into the king's presence, asked David if he had designated Adonijah as the royal heir. At that very moment, Nathan said, a sacrificial banquet was in progress at which all the royal princes but Solomon, who had not been invited, were eating and drinking together with the priest Abiathar and the commander of the army. They were shouting, "Long live King Adonijah!"

At this, David became angry. He shook off his lethargy and promptly made a show of that determination which had been characteristic of him all through his life. Calling Bathsheba to his side, he repeated his oath that Solomon would be king. With resolution he added, "This very day I will fulfill the oath I swore!" (1 Kgs 1:30). He summoned Zadok and Benaiah to join Nathan and ordered Benaiah to mount Solomon on the king's mule and escort him down to Gihon. There Zadok and Nathan were to anoint him king of Israel to the blast of a trumpet and the cry of "Long life King Solomon!" Then they were to come back and Solomon would take his seat on the throne.

They carried out David's orders to the letter, mounting Solomon on the king's mule and escorting him down to Gihon, where Zadok and Nathan took the horn of oil from the tent of the ark and anointed him. And after the blare of the trumpet the people who had assembled there accompanied the new king back up to Zion with pipes playing and exultant cries of "Long live King Solomon!" (1 Kgs 1:40).

By this time, Adonijah's party had finished its festive meal and could not help but hear the uproar. Abiathar's son brought this disturbed assembly the news of what had happened. "Our lord David has made Solomon king!" (1 Kgs 1:43). Solomon was now seated on the royal throne, he said, and the king's officers have all come forward to offer David congratulations. And the old king has bowed down in his bed and thanked the Lord for allowing him to see one of his descendants seated on his throne.

When they had heard this, the conspirators scattered in dismay. Adonijah was terror-stricken. He ran for sanctuary to the altar on Mount Moriah and said that he would not return to Mount Zion unless Solomon swore not to put him to the sword. Solomon merely chided him for the attempted coup, and promised not to harm him as long as he conducted himself as an honorable man. Solomon brought him back from Mount Moriah, received his obeisance, and sent him home.

After Solomon's accession to the throne David charged him to see that justice was done in certain matters outstanding. The murders of Abner and Amasa by Joab were unjustifiable crimes, and were to be avenged on Joab. The sons of Barzillai were to be treated kindly and allowed to dine at the royal table for the sake of their father, who had rescued David when he was fleeing from Absalom. Shimei, who had rained down invectives on the king during that same flight, must be punished for his insults.

David praised God in these words for having blessed him and his House:

Oracle of David son of Jesse,
The utterance of a man whose destiny was
To be the Anointed of Jacob's God,
A singer of the songs of Israel.
Through me the Spirit of God now speaks;
His words take shape upon my lips.
The Almighty, who is just, is the master of men,

Ruling by the fear his name inspires.
He is the light of the dawn at sunrise,
Or the sparkling of the rain freshly fallen on grass.
My House he has made secure and unshaken.
For he made an everlasting Covenant with me,
Something built solid in its every part.
But the wicked are thorns that snag and tear,
Brambles that cannot be taken in hand,
For he who reaches out to take them in his grasp
Soon finds he holds stems with spearpoints like iron.
So let them be burned to a bonfire's ashes. (2 Sm 23:1–7)

David Launches the Temple Project

Though David himself was not to be the one to actually build
the Temple, he had accomplished an immense amount of work in
preparation for it. He had amassed a vast quantity of building
materials, both precious and non-precious. He had drawn up the
structural plans for the Temple in all its various parts and levels,
closely reproducing the master plan for the mobile Temple given
to Moses on Mount Sinai. David designed the sacred furniture—
from the mercy seat, with its cherubim's wings outspread over the
ark, to the lampstands, tables, bowls, forks, and vestments. He had
established the order of the priests and Levites, assigned them
their ritual duties, and set up the rotating schedule according to
which they would serve. In addition, he had composed sacred
psalms and canticles for liturgical use and had designed some
of the musical instruments which would accompany Temple
worship.

David was borne to the throne room, where he had ordered
Israel's most distinguished figures to appear before him. He rose
to his feet and addressed his audience.

I desired to build, as a footstool for our God, a permanent
dwelling for the ark of the Covenant. I made all the provisions
for putting the building up. But God told me, "You may not
construct a house for my name, for you have waged wars and

shed blood." Out of all Israel the Lord had chosen me to reign as king; he had chosen my father's family out of Judah and chosen me out of all the sons of my father. God has now granted me many sons, and out of them has chosen my son Solomon to sit on the throne of Israel. He told me, "It is your son Solomon who shall build my house and my courts, for I have chosen him for my son, and I will be a father to him. I will establish his kingdom forever if he perseveres in keeping my commandments and decrees as he keeps them now." (1 Chr 28:2–7)

David turned to Solomon and continued:

See, then! The Lord has chosen you to build him a house as his sanctuary. Take courage and set to work. Be firm and steadfast; labor without fear of discouragement, for the Lord God, my God, is with you. He will not fail you or abandon you before you have completed everything for the service of the house of the Lord. The priests and Levites are ready; they will help you in all your work, as will all those who are eager to show their skill in every kind of craftsmanship. The leaders and the people will do everything that you command. (1 Chr 28:10, 20–21)

The old king spoke again to the throng assembled there before him and asked for their support. By his own example he challenged them to contribute to the project:

In addition to what I have stored up for the holy Temple, I give to the house of the Lord my personal fortune of gold and silver—3,000 talents of Ophir gold and 7,000 talents of refined silver—for overlaying the walls of the rooms, for the various gold and silver utensils, and for every work that is to be done by artisans. Now, who else is willing to give generously to the Lord this day? (1 Chr 29:3–5)

The heads of families, the leaders of the tribes, the king's administrators, and the officers of the army donated to the Temple treasury 5,000 gold talents, 10,000 gold darics, 10,000 silver tal-

ents, 18,000 bronze talents, and 100,000 iron talents, in addition
to many precious stones. The assembly rejoiced, and David
blessed them. He then blessed God with this prayer:

> O Lord our God, all this wealth that we have brought together
> for the sake of your house comes from you and is entirely yours.
> With a sincere heart I have willingly given my portion, and now
> with joy I have seen your people here also giving to you gener-
> ously. Give to my son Solomon a whole-hearted desire to keep
> your commandments, precepts, and statutes, that he may carry
> out all these plans and build the palace I have prepared. (1 Chr
> 29:16, 17, 19)

Then David exhorted his people:

> Now set to work and start building the sanctuary of the Lord
> your God, so that the ark of the Lord's Covenant and the holy
> things of God can be brought to it. And bless the Lord your
> God! (1 Chr 22:19; 29:20)

The whole assembly blessed the God of their fathers, bowing
down and prostrating themselves before the Lord and before
the king.

The next day, Israel offered holocausts of bulls, rams, and
lambs, a thousand of each, with libations. Then Solomon was
anointed king for the second time, and Zadok was anointed his
priest. All ate and drank joyously in the Lord's presence. Solomon,
sitting on his throne, received a pledge of allegiance from everyone
present, including David's other sons.

Shortly afterward, David reached the end of his life. When he
fell asleep on Mount Zion and went to join his ancestors he was
seventy years of age. He had been thirty years old when he ascended the throne, and he was king for forty years. He ruled from
Hebron as king of Judah for seven years and six months; then he
reigned in Jerusalem over all of Israel and Judah for thirty-three
years. If the year 1000 B.C. is taken as the approximate, probable
date for the start of David's reign, then his birth may be placed
at about 1031 B.C. and his death at about 960 B.C.

Recapitulation of the Man and his Reign

To see David for what he really was, let us consider him first as a historical figure, and then as a very human individual.

David son of Jesse came into view as a shepherd boy of about sixteen years of age. He was a brave, active, and resourceful lad who had fought and killed lions and bears preying upon his father's flocks. He came to the attention of all Israel when he brought down the giant Philistine warrior Goliath on the battlefield by using only his slingshot. Later David won such acclaim and popularity for his military exploits that King Saul became envious of him and sought to kill him. As a young man in his twenties, he was forced to flee from the king, hiding in the mountains of Judah until compelled to seek uncertain refuge in the Philistine foothills. At Saul's death, David was called to occupy the throne of his native tribe of Judah. At that time he was thirty years old. Seven and a half years later, David became king of the whole nation, and he besieged and took Jerusalem for his capital. He put down all of Israel's foes, and administered the empire that he had conquered.

David cherished a desire to build a great Temple for the Lord. He collected materials for the edifice from his subject peoples, and assembled artisans and other workers to help prepare for its construction. Although God forbade him to actually build the Temple himself, he nevertheless made the necessary arrangements for the entire project, drawing up the definitive plans for the Temple's design and making an effective appeal for contributions to the Temple treasury. He instituted the choral worship of the Temple and personally composed psalms for its hymnbook. And as David's days drew near their end, he saw to it that his son Solomon was enthroned after him.

Many historians see in David the greatest king to ever rule Israel, as the one who gave unity and stability to the nation that Moses had created, who founded an empire which stretched from the Wadi of Egypt to the Pass at Hamath and the Euphrates, and who made Hebrew power dominant in the Middle East of that day.

Consider next how appealingly human an individual this great personage was. Even as a youth David had a gift for music, for with his harp he was able to soothe the fitfulness of moody King Saul. His close friendship with Jonathan knit their souls together in a love that reached beyond the grave to bestow kindnesses on Jonathan's son and grandson. As a young man fallen from royal favor, David was a fugitive who tirelessly bore up under all the obstacles that Saul put in his way. Though persecuted as an outcast by Saul, he nevertheless forgave the king and showed him an unfailing, reverential regard as the Anointed of the Lord. He was the bard who sang a dirge at the news of Saul's and Jonathan's deaths, calling them heroes "swifter than eagles and stronger than lions" (2 Sm 1:29).

As a general, David was able to inspire such great devotion and loyalty in his men that some of them risked their lives to fight through an enemy-held position simply to bring him a cup of water. He was a wily leader who side-stepped Israelite betrayals, while making game of the Philistine foe, once even beguiling an enemy king into taking him for a madman.

David was every bit as human as he was great. He could sway his nation as easily as he directed the armies under his command. He loved beauty and was snared by the loveliness of Bathsheba; carried away by this attraction, he was responsible for the murder of her husband. Yet he mournfully prayed against the death prophesied for the child of his adultery right up to the moment the baby died. As a father he was indulgent to a fault with his sons, and found himself unable to chastize Amnon, Absalom, or Adonijah for their crimes.

David was kind to Meribaal and Barzillai; forgiving but not forgetful of the insults of Shimei; appreciative of Joab's military prowess yet careful to insure his punishment for the murders he committed. Supremely devoted to God, David was conscious that every man, no matter how exalted his earthly station, is answerable to the Lord. He loved God deeply and wrote songs of praise to him. He danced round the ark without shame and desired with all his heart to build a magnificent dwelling to be God's house. In a word, he was musician, psalmist, conqueror, and far-famed ruler all in one.

Four years after David's death, Solomon laid the Temple's foundations. His work on the Temple took seven years to complete. Then the ark, with the stone tablets, was brought there from Gihon, and the tent of meeting with its sacred vessels transferred there from Gibeon. The Temple's solemn dedication took place on the feast of Tabernacles, probably in 949 B.C.

David's life and works were never to be forgotten. Almost 800 years later, Ben Sira says of King David:

Like the choice fat of the sacred offerings set apart from the flesh in holocausts and peace offerings, so was David in Israel. With his every deed he offered thanks in words of praise to God Most High, and with his whole being he loved his maker and daily had his praises sung. He gave beauty to the feasts and solemnized the seasons of each year. The music of the harp before the altar provided sweet melody for the psalms, so that when the holy name was praised before daybreak, the sanctuary would resound. (Sir 47:2, 8–10)

CANAAN BEFORE THE CONQUEST

Copyright by C. S. HAMMOND & CO., N. Y.

Scale of Miles

0 5 10   20   30   40

Perennial Rivers
Capitals ....

HITTITE EMPIRE Ubi

Damascus

Sidon

Phoenicians from the cities of Sidon and Tyre traded throughout the Mediterranean

Zarephath

Tyre

Kanah

Laish (Dan)

Kedesh

Misrephoth-maim

Hazor

Achzib

Merom

BASHAN (KINGDOM OF OG)

Accho

Achshaph

Chinnereth

Karnaim

Ashtaroth

Madon

Sea of Chinnereth

Yarmuk R.

The Great Sea

(Mediterranean Sea)

MT. CARMEL

Shimron

Jokneam

Mt. Tabor

Edrei

Dor

Megiddo

Taanach

Ham

Ramoth-gilead

Ibleam

Beth-shan

Dothan

Pella

Jabesh-gilead

Mahanaim

The 13th and 12th century kingdoms of Bashan, Ammon, Moab and Edom displaced the Rephaim, Zuzim, Emim and Horites respectively.

Tirzah

Mt. Ebal

Shechem

Jacob's Well

Mt. Gerizim

Succoth

Penuel (Peniel)

Aphek

Tappuah

Adam

Joppa

Ono

Lod

Jazer

Rabbath-ammon

AMMON

Canaan at this time was an Egyptian province organized on a city-state system. The local kings were only required to pay tribute and to furnish labor for Egyptian royal projects.

Bethel

Ai

Gezer

Beeroth

Ekron

Gibeon

Jericho

Chephirah

Gilgal

Kirjath-jearim

Heshbon

Ashdod

Beth-shemesh

Jerusalem (Jebus, Salem)

Mt. Nebo (Pisgah)

Medeba

Makkedah

Jarmuth

Bethlehem

Ashkelon

Libnah

Adullam

Gath

Jahaz

Gaza (Azzah)

Eglon

Lachish

Kirjath-arba (Hebron)

Memre

Kiriathaim

Dibon

Gerar

Kirjath-sepher (Debir)

Hazeon-tamar (En-gedi)

Aroer

Raphia

Arad

Ar

Sharuhen

Beer-sheba

Kir-moab (Kir-haresheth)

Hormah

MOAB

Amalekites

The destroyed cities of Sodom and Gomorrah are believed to be beneath the shallow waters of the Dead Sea which now cover the Vale of Siddim (shaded portion).

Rehoboth

Zoar

Ascent of Akrabbim

Wilderness of Zin

Bozrah

Kadesh-barnea (En-mishpat)

Oboth

EDOM

Punon

Salt Sea (Dead Sea)

River Jordan

AMORITES KINGDOM OF SIHON

Plains of Moab

River of Egypt

THE ROUTE OF THE EXODUS AND
THE CONQUEST OF CANAAN

Copyright by C. S. HAMMOND & CO., N.Y.

Scale of Miles

0   20   40   60   80   100

Perennial Rivers ....
Seasonal Rivers & Streams
Capitals ....
Trade Routes ....
Traditional Route of the Exodus ....→
Israelite Campaigns in Canaan ......⇢
Israelite Expansion & Settlement

The Great Sea
(Mediterranean Sea)

HITTITE
EMPIRE
Ubi
Damascus

Joshua defeated the allied
kings of northern Canaan at the
Battle by the Waters of Merom.

Egypt exercised loose control over Canaan at this time.

After the fall of Jericho
Joshua conquered central
and southern Canaan.

Egyptian forts near the
coast barred the direct route
to Canaan to the Israelites.

In the land of
Goshen the Israelites
dwelt in bondage.

Possible sites of the
crossing of the Red Sea
(The Sea of Reeds).

Israelites wandered in the
wilderness for a generation.
Exact route unknown.

Israel's enemy, the
Amalekites, wandered
as nomads between
Canaan and Mt. Sinai.

Traditional site where
Moses received the Ten
Commandments.

Nile Delta

GOSHEN

Rameses or Zoan (Tanis)
Baal-zephon
Sin (Pelusium)
L. Ballah
Pithom
Succoth
On (Heliopolis)
Etham
Memphis
Pyramids
Heracleopolis
Lycopolis

E G Y P T
(M I Z R A I M)

Wilderness of Shur

Jebel Helal

River of Egypt

Wilderness of Etham

Gulf of Suez

Marah

Elim

Wilderness of Sin

SINAI
PENINSULA

Dophkah

Alush

Rephidim

Mt. Horeb

Jebel Serbal

Kibroth-hattaavah
Hazeroth

Taberah

Wilderness
of Paran

Kadesh-barnea

Wilderness
of Zin

Beer-sheba

Hormah?

Unsuccessful
invasion

Ezion-geber
Elath

Gulf of Aqaba

LAND

OF

MIDIAN

Red Sea

Bitter
Lakes

Temah

CANAAN

Sidon
Tyre
Laish (Dan)
Kedesh
Merom
Misrephoth-maim
Hazor
Accho
Madon
Shimron
Dor
Megiddo
Mt. Carmel
Beth-shan
Shechem
Mt. Ebal
Mt. Gerizim
Shiloh
Joppa
Aphek
Gibeon Ai
Ashdod
Makkedah
Gilgal
Jericho
Jerusalem (Jebus)
Gezer
Libnah
Jarmuth
Ashkelon
Gath
Lachish
Hebron
Gaza (Azzah)
Eglon
Debir

BASHAN
(OG)
Ashtaroth
Edrei

Sea of
Chinnereth

Mt. Hermon

Gilead

Jordan

Jabbok

Jazer
Rabbath-ammon
Heshbon

Mt. Nebo
(Pisgah)

Jahaz

AMMON

Dibon

Salt
(Dead)
Sea

Ar
Kir-moab

MOAB

Zoar

ije-abarim

Oboth

Bozrah

Punon

Mt. Hor
(Jebel Harun)

Arabah

EDOM

GREAT DESERT